BORN TO RISE

BORN TO RISE

A STORY OF CHILDREN AND TEACHERS
REACHING THEIR HIGHEST POTENTIAL

* * * * * * * *

Deborah Kenny

HARPER

An Imprint of HarperCollins*Publishers*
www.harpercollins.com

HarperCollins books may be purchased for educational, business, or sales promotional use. For information, please write: Special Markets Department, HarperCollins Publishers, 10 East 53rd Street, New York, NY 10022.

Grateful acknowledgment is made for permission to reprint from the following:

Excerpt from "Little Gidding" Part V in *Four Quartets*, copyright 1942 by T. S. Eliot and renewed in 1970 by Esme Valerie Eliot, reprinted by permission of Houghton Mifflin Harcourt Publishing Company and Faber and Faber Ltd. All rights reserved.

Harlem Village Academies' school song is reprinted with the permission of John Legend.

All photos courtesy of Harlem Village Academies, with the exception of the photo of the author on *Sesame Street*: Sesame Street® and related characters, trademarks, and design elements are owned by Sesame Workshop. Copyright © 1999 Sesame Workshop. All rights reserved.

FIRST EDITION

Designed by Lisa Stokes

Library of Congress Cataloging-in-Publication Data has been applied for.

ISBN: 978-0-06-210620-9

12 13 14 15 16   OV/RRD   10 9 8 7 6 5 4 3

AUTHOR'S NOTE

Three years ago, a good friend convinced me that it was finally time to respond to the question I'm most frequently asked: why did you start Harlem Village Academies? In so doing, I did not set out to write a personal memoir, yet it became clear that certain aspects of my personal life would need to be included to elucidate the journey of the last ten years. For every story I've shared here, there are a hundred I haven't shared—and hundreds of heroes as well as life experiences that are not included. Some conversations and events have been condensed for clarity, and in some instances I have changed the names and/or identifying characteristics of individuals to protect their privacy, including students, parents, and some teachers, principals, colleagues, and others.

For My Children

CONTENTS

BORN TO RISE

CHAPTER 1

SEARCHING

"OKAY, READY FOR YOUR THREE CLUES?" he asked. "This country starts with a *V* and it's in South America. The capital is Caracas and the people speak Spanish."

It was another round of "Kenny family geography," a game my husband, Joel, had invented to keep our three young kids busy during car rides.

"That's four clues!" shouted Rachel, our youngest, then age six.

"The first letter of the country doesn't count," our eight-year-old, Chava, stated firmly. "We get that for free."

"It's Venzulia!" fired Avi, nine, and very much the oldest.

"Nice try, Av," said Joel from behind the wheel. "You're close."

"Trust me, Dad, it's *Venzulia*," Avi repeated emphatically.

Suddenly we heard a lot of shrieking and giggling as our three children began another game they liked even better. They called it "boxing," but they were actually just playfully hitting each other.

"Knock it off!" Joel said, grinning. "Avi, I told you that you're close. Think about it."

"Dad, I'm going to ask you one last time. *Is it Venzulia?*"

Joel and I burst out laughing.

It was a golden Sunday in June of 1998, and we were headed to a science museum in Connecticut. The kids had been looking forward to this trip for weeks. They'd been eager to see the exhibit about marine biology ever since we'd rented a video about whales the month before.

We zipped north along the Saw Mill River Parkway in Westchester, New York—just twenty more minutes, I told the kids—when Joel said he felt a bit dizzy. We figured it was the flu.

But the next morning Joel felt even fainter—strange for a guy who never complained and never got sick—so I drove him to a doctor, just to check.

The doctor ran a few blood tests and said he'd be back shortly with the results. A half hour went by. Then a full hour.

Finally, the doctor came back into the room. "I don't want to alarm you," he said softly, "but this could be serious. Joel, there is a chance you have a leukemic condition."

He tried to keep us calm. "Nothing is definite yet. But you need to have a spinal tap."

We drove back home and I started making calls to figure out what to do. As I arranged an appointment for the next day, Joel lay very still on the bed staring at the ceiling. Just looking at him, so silent and scared, devastated me. But I tried not to let that show. "The tests will come back negative," I said, holding his hand. "All of this will be over tomorrow."

That night, it was impossible to sleep. I spent the dark hours before sunrise praying silently, asking God to protect Joel.

The next morning we drove to Mount Sinai Hospital in Manhattan for the spinal tap. It was an excruciating procedure, but it was the only way to figure out exactly what was wrong, and it had to be done immediately. I sat by his side as we breathed together the whole time, holding hands. When it was finally done, we expected to go home. Instead, the specialist sent us to the third floor.

Joel and I didn't acknowledge the two words that accosted us when we stepped off the elevator: "Oncology Unit." As we waited in an empty room, I was petrified but I buried that feeling. Instead, I tried to distract Joel with questions about his dissertation and he tried to distract me with jokes.

Suddenly, some ten doctors, nurses, and residents swarmed the room. I stopped breathing. The doctor looked straight into our eyes, and spoke immediately: "I'm sorry, Joel. You have leukemia."

Joel was the person in the world I most admired, one of those rare individuals born to a higher purpose. I was enchanted by him from the moment we met.

I was twenty-four years old and had just ended a relationship with a Harvard law student who was smart, ambitious, and good-looking. But I hadn't connected with him on a deep level. I was hoping to meet someone with soul.

Within half an hour of our first date, Joel and I were discussing spirituality. As we walked around Greenwich Village in lower Manhattan, I learned that he played guitar, loved nature, painted, and was a Dallas Cowboys fan. The four Kenny brothers, he explained, played football almost every day in their backyard as kids, and they never missed a Cowboys game.

Joel, quiet but confident, was not intimidated by me. His mother, Shirley, was a college president who had worked full-time as an English professor while raising five children in McLean, Virginia, with Joel's father, a history professor.

In between our dates, he wrote me love letters with pink hearts hand-drawn in colored pencil on the envelopes. Before long we started talking about the future. He told me about his desire to teach, to write books, to have a big family, and to compose his own music. I was falling in love.

Like me, Joel had studied religion and philosophy in college. I'd never been with another person who thought debating the nature of Truth was an ideal way to spend a Saturday night.

For as far back as I can remember, I'd been this way. In high school, my parents worried that I was too serious. They encouraged me to try more activities, to lighten up, to "be well rounded." My response was to write an editorial—"The Myth of the Well Rounded Child"—in the school newspaper, in which I argued that it was more valuable to pursue one thing intensely than to participate in a wide variety of school activities.

I didn't fit into any clique, and I didn't care much about being popular. I spent prom night with Sara, one of my best friends, talking in her kitchen and eating tuna melts.

The summer camp Sara and I attended was a welcome change from the superficiality of high school. While the kids loved to socialize and have fun, it was the kind of place where it was cool to be smart and everyone fit in. The camp was dedicated to Jewish values and social justice. The chorus of our camp song was "You and I will change the world"—and everyone actually believed it, including me. It was bliss.

It was at camp where I met the teacher who would change my life: Mel Reisfeld. He was an extraordinary and often irreverent educator, and for many decades the camp's heart and soul. He was the coolest adult we kids had ever met. Mel could captivate hundreds of campers and counselors for hours with lectures about history, heritage, and social justice. My favorite stories were about his activism—how in 1963, he got in a car with a friend and two students and drove to D.C. for the March on Washington to hear Dr. Martin Luther King Jr.; how he led efforts to raise funds for Biafra when Africans were starving; how he had helped organize one of the very first walkathons for the March of Dimes; and how he joined in protests to support farm labor leader César Chávez. "We have to care about people," he would always say. Mel also loved to provoke us. One night at dinner he gave eight of us the following challenge: "How many of you know how to say 'fuck' in another language?" We tried to impress him with our linguistic skills for the next hour.

Despite—or perhaps because of—his irreverence, Mel was a role model for the other counselors, many of whom had been activists in the 1960s. They were all, like Mel, independent thinkers who challenged societal norms. I related to their worldview: challenging the establishment made immediate sense to me.

One of my camp counselors introduced me to brown rice, juice fasting, and yoga. My mother was beside herself when at age fourteen I decided to become a vegetarian. "What about protein?" she worried. "The idea that protein is more important than other nutrients is a myth perpetuated by the meat and dairy industries," I assured her. This was the late 1970s, when "health food" was considered bizarre. I didn't care that everyone thought I was a bit nuts.

By junior year of high school, I felt even more disconnected from my peers. The pursuit of success seemed trivial to me. Instead, I was drawn to the discussions I'd had at camp about religion and social justice. I started keeping a journal and collecting quotes that inspired me. "A shallow mind is a sin, a person who does not struggle is a fool," I copied down from Chaim Potok's book *In the Beginning*.

And in my senior year I started writing down the questions that were on my mind: What is the meaning of life? Being happy is great, but is being happy a purpose in and of itself? What's my plan for the future? I'll pick a major to get a job to work my way up, to get a better job to be promoted to . . . then what? In twenty years I'll be exactly where I am now, wondering what it was all for. What's my ultimate purpose?

My mom threw a big party for my high school graduation. In our living room with a house full of family and friends she recited a poem that she had written in my honor. "If a woman does not keep pace with her companions," it started, "perhaps it is because she hears a different drummer." I felt lucky to have such supportive parents.

At the University of Pennsylvania, I spent a lot of time at coffee shops, stacks of books piled before me, talking late into the night with friends about the meaning of life. Early freshman year, I had discovered Rainer Maria Rilke. I must have read *Letters to a Young Poet* a hundred times. "Nobody can counsel and help you—no one. There is only one single way," Rilke wrote. "Go into yourself. Search . . . Dig into yourself for a deep answer. And if this answer rings out true, if you meet this solemn question with a strong and simple, 'I must,' then build your life according to this necessity. Your whole life, even into its slightest and most indifferent hour, must be a sign of this urge and a testimony to it." What would my life be a testimony to, I wondered.

My advisor allowed me to craft an independent major that enabled me to explore comparative religion, literature, and philosophy—and I was thrilled. My father wasn't. He'd been pushing the doctor/lawyer track since I was in grade school. "What are you going to do?" he asked. "Open a philosophy store?"

I had no idea what I'd do with it, but I didn't care. I just wanted to find answers to my questions.

My favorite course was American Intellectual History. It was listed as a senior seminar, limited to twelve students. I was a sophomore when I walked into the room, and it was overflowing with almost fifty students, standing in every corner, some huddled near the door.

"I'm so sorry," the professor said, "but we are oversubscribed. Will everyone who is a junior please raise your hand." Some twenty students raised their hands, and the professor apologetically asked them to come back the next year. He then asked any of the remaining seniors who were not fully committed to consider leaving, and another dozen walked out of the room. Fifteen students remained, including me.

"The course structure will be the same each week," he said. "You will read a book and write a paper grappling with the author's ideas. When you arrive to class, be prepared to defend your understanding of the text. You *will* be called on."

I knew that it would not be long before the professor looked at his roster and discovered that I was a sophomore. But I was dying to study the works of great American thinkers like Thoreau, Emerson, and the other Transcendentalists. I admired their rebellion against the intellectual establishment of their time and I was fascinated by their idealistic spiritual quest. Emerson had written about the "endless inquiry of the intellect"—I *had* to be in this class!

So I spent fifteen hours writing a paper that week, and made an appointment to meet with the professor.

"I asked to see you because I want to let you know that I am a sophomore," I admitted in his office. "Even though you didn't require a paper this first week, I wrote one to show you how committed I am, how much I want to take this course." He told me I could stay that day, and he would make a final decision the following week.

When I arrived the next week, the professor handed me back my unrequired paper. On the front was a red C-. "You can stay," he said. "But do better next time." I was in heaven.

I spent many evenings in the library. One Sunday as I was walking along the brick path from my dorm to the library I stopped right in the middle of campus and wondered: if I were able to read every book in the library, would I then understand Truth?

On weekends I'd end up in long conversations in dorm rooms with other students, but I spent much more time with adults: my Shakespeare professor, the campus rabbi, my dorm advisor Dr. Martin Seligman. And with a grad student I'd met at the only health food store on campus who told me that Ram Dass, the counterculture icon and author of *Be Here Now*, was coming to Philadelphia.

Ram Dass, originally named Richard Alpert, had been a prominent Harvard professor when he experimented with LSD in the early 1960s with Aldous Huxley, Allen Ginsberg, and Timothy Leary. Though he justified it as research into the nature of human consciousness, Harvard kicked him out—and countless kids got turned on to his message. I had no interest in drugs, but I was very interested in the ideas that he espoused.

I arrived early to a packed auditorium. Ram Dass addressed all of the things I had been thinking about. "What am I doing here?" he asked. "Who are you? What is God?" He spoke about the illusion of separateness, and transcending the rational mind's limitations through meditation. "Somewhere along the line you realize you aren't who you thought you were." He quoted Einstein, Kabbalah, Confucius, a Tibetan lama, Ramana Maharshi, and a Benedictine monk. "In the sixties," he said, "we used to think strong people are rational and analytic, weak people and women are intuitive. But look how it turned out! *Isn't it far out?*"

I had taped the lecture with a small recorder, and when I got back to my dorm room I transcribed it into my journal. As I was writing, my friends Robert and Jon walked in and asked what I was doing. We stayed up all night as I told them what Ram Dass had said. It all made sense to me, much more so than the life I had experienced growing up.

Not that there had been anything wrong with my childhood: I was raised by loving parents. My mom was a homemaker and freelance journalist and my dad was briefly a schoolteacher, then a stockbroker. They gave me a tremendous amount of freedom, and knowing that they would do anything for me gave me confidence and stability. Still, I just always felt like there was more to life than financial or career achievement.

When my mom and dad came to visit me in college one weekend, I was sitting in my dorm room with a few friends. "What are you studying?" my mother asked, looking skeptically at the books on my shelf. She'd brought me another copy of Ayn Rand's *Atlas Shrugged*, just in case I had misplaced the copy she had given me the year before. "What are you kids doing tonight?" my father asked my friends, embarrassing me as usual. "We're going to a party," they replied. "Make sure to take Debbie with you," he said. My friends laughed. "She doesn't go to parties."

After my friends left, he immediately turned to me, "Go with them, Debbie! You'll have fun! What's wrong with a little socializing?" I brushed him off. "It's boring," I replied. "It's just music, drinking, and people." My parents started cracking up. "What's so funny?" I asked. "That's what a party is!" they replied.

But I had no interest. Instead, I typed other students' papers for a dollar a page. I wanted to save enough money to take the train to Boston during winter break to meet raw foods pioneer Ann Wigmore. We met in her apartment and she introduced me to sprouts and wheatgrass juice. Then, during spring break that year, I found my way to a farm in Woodstock, Connecticut, where I spent a week in a cabin on a lake with Ann's colleague, another pioneer of raw foods, Viktoras Kulvinskas, and a dozen of their friends. I had read two of his books and wanted to learn more. "Realize there is life in everything," he wrote. "Realize you are not what you've been taught. Allow consciousness to unite with you. And some day, we won't stop smiling. When we walk, we'll float. And light will pour from our eyes." I spent the week eating sprouts, learning meditation, and hanging upside down every morning from ropes on the ceiling.

As intrigued as I was by these practices, part of me remained skeptical. Some of the people I met were serious thinkers, but some, quite clearly, were quacks. The healthy-eating aspect of it stayed with me, but I became increasingly unimpressed with what I considered a shallow and somewhat self-centered approach to spirituality. I believed religion and spirituality had to be less about attaining enlightenment—perfecting oneself—and more about subordinating oneself and sacrificing for the greater good.

What I enjoyed more than anything was being with my friends from camp. So every summer for a few years I worked as a camp counselor. I asked Mel to place me in his group—he was *the* senior counselor and everyone wanted to work for him and learn about leadership.

And being at camp allowed me plenty of time to read and to talk with my friends about Emerson, Kabbalah, and William James. I'd often talk with my friend Steve while listening to him playing guitar. If you study religion deeply enough, I asked one day, don't you think eventually it will lead to understanding Truth? "It depends. Which religion?" Steve asked. "They're all so different."

On the surface, Steve was right—all religions seemed quite different. But at a deeper level, I'd discovered that the mystical teachings were similar. I thought about a poem by T. S. Eliot that I had posted inside my bunk at the beginning of the summer, "We shall not cease from exploration / And the end of all our exploring / Will be to arrive where we started / And know the place for the first time." Maybe that was it. Maybe I needed to take one path and follow it as far as it would go. I would study my own religion more intensely— not because it was truer than any other, but because I already knew about it, and if I went deep enough, maybe I could come to understand the universe.

"Mail call!" exclaimed Diane, the camper in charge of mail for the week. She had a letter for me from Semester at Sea, a program for college students to study abroad on a boat trip around the world. I had completely forgotten that I had applied. And now I had just been accepted.

"That is so cool!" Diane yelled. A few of my friends gathered around.

"You are so lucky!" said my friend David.

"Wow, you get course credit for this?"

"What countries will you get to see?"

I tucked the letter inside my journal. "I'm not going," I said to them.

"What do you mean?" Diane asked.

"I need to explore the inner world, not the outer world," I said. "I'm going to spend a semester meditating and studying Kabbalah in Israel."

"Well, now it's official," said David. "You've lost your fucking mind!"

That next semester, I studied mysticism from dawn to dusk. At first, it was incredibly exciting. We would meditate, pray, and attend classes all morning, then read for hours in the afternoon. I would stay up late every night with our group, talking as we looked out on the thousand-year-old mountains and ancient caves. But eventually I felt that I'd come up against a wall: understanding the universe was infinitely impossible. "The more I learn," I wrote in my journal, "the more I realize how much I don't know. The world of knowledge is so vast. I'll never get there."

I went to the library to talk with the school's rabbi. He was an amazing teacher: unassuming, modest, and brilliant. "I've spent several years trying to understand the purpose of life," I said. "But now I'm realizing how insignificant my life is in the grand scheme of things." He smiled calmly. "That's a very useful stage," he said. "When you realize that you do not matter, all of a sudden there are all these other people who do matter. Life is about service to others. I mean—*what else is there?*"

I walked straight back to the dorm, took my journal out of the top drawer, and sat still for a moment. After years of searching, I had come to a conclusion. As I considered what he said, and as I thought about the massive amount of human suffering in the world, I realized that contemplating philosophy all this time had been a luxury. I had found the meaning I had been searching for in the simple idea of using my life in service to others. "I thought I had come up against a wall," I wrote. "It turns out, it was a door."

In Joel, for the first time, I found a spiritual partner who saw things the same way. He had studied religion and philosophy, and had explored the same kinds of ideas in college, and he'd come to many of the same conclusions as I had. He was my perfect match.

When we got married in 1987, I had recently started a doctoral program at Columbia University's Teachers College; Joel would soon pursue his doctorate in medieval mysticism downtown at New York University.

My first assignment in graduate school was to write about my educational philosophy. My essay was titled "Becoming an Educator." To me, education was about shaping students' worldview and character. "In its highest form, education means being an embodiment of the message one wishes to communicate," I wrote. "Rather than imposing ideas on the student, the true teacher creates a framework within which the student may make something of himself."

When I enrolled, I hadn't fully realized that Teachers College was a bastion of liberal views. (I had started the same year as former Weather Underground member Bill Ayers, although he was twenty years older than me.) Maxine Greene, the celebrated education philosopher, was one of my favorite professors. She believed that the purpose of education was to help students understand their connection to, and responsibility for, all of humanity. Professor Greene and virtually everyone I encountered felt that the role of educators was to inspire and empower students to become critical thinkers who contribute to a democratic and compassionate society.

I was deeply enamored with these ideals, and I asked Professor Greene to be my thesis advisor. I loved every aspect of Teachers College: taking courses in comparative education, student teaching in Brooklyn, and learning about curriculum planning.

Meanwhile, I had three babies by the time I was twenty-nine. Over the course of ten years, between raising them while holding various jobs to pay the bills, I worked my way through graduate school.

I had considered becoming a public school principal after completing my degree, but a professor talked me out of that. "You wouldn't last a minute in a bureaucracy," she said. I hadn't yet heard about charter schools, and none existed in New York. "So what if I start private schools for underserved communities?" I had suggested. "Then you won't be an educator—you'll spend ninety-nine percent of your time worrying about money," she said.

I didn't know what to do. Then a friend told me about a career planning workshop and I signed up. After a full day of exercises, the leader sat down with me. "All seven indicators show clearly you have a business mind, but your heart wants to work with children or parents. So why not combine those and look into companies that make children's products—maybe books or toys?" That sounded interesting. So I set out to meet with companies like Scholastic, Stride Rite, Hasbro, and *Parenting* magazine.

The summer before our kids started kindergarten and first and second grade, we decided to move to Westchester to take advantage of the quality public schools. We also wanted our children to have a moral education, so for two hours on Sunday mornings and Tuesday and Thursday afternoons, they went to religious school. Late one Sunday afternoon, I overheard Avi and Chava talking in the family room. "Will you please share your Legos with me?" he asked her. "No," she said without looking up. "But God says we're supposed to share," he offered. "No, I don't want to," she replied. "But if you don't share, I'm gonna kill you." Okay, so they weren't saints!

Sunday night was family reading night—I would spread out a blanket in the living room, make a big bowl of popcorn, and we'd all spend the night reading while listening to Vivaldi. In the winter, we would get a fire going, but in the summer, the kids would always end up outside playing hide-and-seek or catching fireflies with their neighborhood friends.

I had a definite sense of the values I wanted to impart, and went about parenting by doing things in a deliberate way. I taught the children from a very young age to give to charity; I explained that they should give until they were slightly uncomfortable or had to miss out on something. I signed up our family to participate in an interfaith sandwich-making project for the homeless, and took the kids to classical music concerts each winter at Lincoln Center and Carnegie Hall.

Joel went about parenting by always making the kids his first priority. He had infinite patience: even when he was in the middle of writing, he would drop his work the moment one of them asked for something—to work in the garden, help with a science project, or fix a toy. He was kind and intellectually curious, and the kids naturally absorbed those qualities. And he spoke to them the same way he spoke to adults, with a dry wit that made me laugh all the time.

In the summer of 1998, he was just a few months away from defending his dissertation. Now those three words from the doctor— "I'm sorry, Joel"—had devastated him.

In the hospital, while the nurses took him for more blood tests, the oncologist approached me. "Joel needs to start chemo immediately. He could die in a matter of days if we do not begin treatment."

"Okay, I'll put off the start date for my new job. About how long is the treatment?" I asked the doctor. I had just been hired by Time Warner as vice president of marketing and business development for The Parenting Group, which published *Parenting* magazine. In addition to marketing, I would be responsible for developing products for new mothers and their children.

"It's going to be a very long road," said the doctor. "You definitely should start the job." I couldn't imagine doing that.

"But he needs me," I replied.

"He's going to need you more later. You have to take care of yourself, take care of your kids, and keep your job."

"I just can't see myself going to work," I said. The doctor was sympathetic but adamant. "Someone has to support the family. He could be in treatment for one or two years." As the doctor spoke, tears started streaming down my face.

"You are going through what everyone goes through at this time," he said.

The next day, Joel's parents, who had been at a conference in Greece, arrived along with his brothers and sister from Washington, D.C. We filled them in on all that had transpired. With everyone gathered around his hospital bed, Joel started making jokes as he always did. The nurses had already identified him as their favorite patient. "It's time for your EKG," one of them said. "I'd rather have a K–E–G," he replied. Another nurse came by to bring his lunch. "Has anyone died? Maybe then I'd get my food faster," he deadpanned. And on it went.

I had no previous experience with hospitals but I quickly learned the ropes. I became an advocate for Joel's needs, the most important of which was sleep. I would stay half-awake all night sitting up in a chair that I positioned at the foot of his bed, facing the door. This way, when a nurse entered I would indicate to her that she should whisper, and suggest that she didn't need to turn on a light in order to take Joel's temperature. It was amazing how nurses would walk in with a booming voice yelling "How are we doing?" at two-thirty in the morning. "He's sleeping," I would say, always smiling and whispering, hoping they would realize he should not be woken up every two hours.

We had told our children that Daddy was sick, but we hadn't given any details. On a Saturday in July, shortly after the diagnosis, I brought them to visit him. The minute he saw the children, his eyes became misty. But he put on an outward display of brightness for their sake.

When it was time to go, I told the kids to sit on the chairs in the hall for a minute. As soon as they walked out of the room, Joel started sobbing. "I need to be here for them," he said.

"You will. You'll get through this and everything is going to be fine," I said, holding both his hands. "I'll be back tomorrow morning. I'll call you tonight."

"I love you," he said.

"I love you, too. This will all be over soon. I promise."

CHAPTER 2

WHAT LIFE EXPECTS

I FORCED MYSELF TO GO TO my new job on the first day.

"Welcome!" chirped the highly caffeinated receptionist. "We've been looking forward to you joining us. Michael is expecting you."

As I walked into his office, Michael was brimming with energy. "Thrilled to have you here, Deborah. This is going to be the beginning of something big," he said. "The Parenting Group is more than a magazine; it's a brand. We have enormous potential for synergy and new product lines."

I wondered what Joel was doing in the hospital that morning. Probably reading one of his books for his dissertation. Maybe he's sleeping. What if he's bored? I wonder if he's thirsty, if he ate anything for breakfast. God, I need to get out of here at five-thirty so that I can squeeze in an hour with him before I go home to the kids. Maybe I should bring him some crossword puzzles . . .

"Corporate has given me the latitude to build something, and they're willing to invest in us," Michael continued. "You'll have the freedom to come up with product ideas and run with them," he said. "But there are a few things you should know," he said slowly, staring right at me.

I hadn't been listening, and it showed. I didn't care about *Parenting* magazine's corporate plans, but I had a responsibility to my family. They needed me to do this job. "There are a few things I should know?" I offered enthusiastically.

Michael began to explain the internal politics of the company, which could undermine my success. "Brad wanted you to report to him, and Ellen wanted you to report to her. But I decided you were reporting to me, so neither of them is thrilled." It would have been nice to know this before my first day, I thought to myself. "They'll get over it," he said. "Just wanted to give you a heads-up."

When I sat down at my desk and logged on to my computer, my first email was one that Michael had forwarded to me with nothing more than "FYI" as the subject line. The original email was from Brad, pitching Michael on all the reasons he should be in charge of everything that was now my responsibility. As if on cue, Brad walked into my office. I scrambled to close the email. "I wanted to be the first to welcome you! Hope everything is going well," he said with a smile. "Good so far," I said.

Next I went down the hall to say hello to Ellen. She was smart and brash and could be tough with her criticism, but I admired her assertiveness. "It would be great to hear about your goals, so we can work together effectively," I said after I walked in. She didn't get up and didn't offer me a seat. "You are Michael's hire, not mine," she said. "I need marketing to report directly to me."

I was a very long way from Teachers College. I had never worked in a corporate environment before and I had no experience with office politics. But I didn't have the luxury of doing a bad job: we needed the income and the health insurance and I had a responsibility to make it work.

Meantime, Joel had lots of visitors at the hospital, and his father became his primary caregiver. I did my best to keep everything as normal as possible for the kids.

Despite the pain, the exhaustion, and the lack of privacy, Joel insisted on being himself. One day after a particularly difficult round of chemo, he decided to write "The Pros and Cons of Dying":

Pro: People are nicer to you.

Con: You die at the end.

Pro: For once, the funeral doesn't interfere with your schedule.

Con: After that, your schedule's pretty dead.

Pro: Nobody asks, "So, when are you going to finish that Ph.D.?"

Con: No beer.

Pro: Could it be that much worse than Brooklyn?

Con: Miss a lot of Super Bowls.

Pro: Not really worried about the ozone layer.

Con: No Victoria's Secret catalogues.

Over the next few months, I tried to put office politics out of my mind and focus on doing what I was hired to do. My job was to come up with new products for parents to help them raise wholesome children, and I was excited about that mission.

I had a great team—they were sharp, energetic, and professional. As we brainstormed new product ideas, I asked them to think on two levels: profits and purpose. Many of the team members were inspired by this approach to new business development, but others thought it was too touchy-feely. "Mothers of young children are educating the next generation," I told them. "If we can influence them, we can make a difference."

One of the project managers, a warm, kind woman named Carol, was particularly interested. We'd often talk about our shared concern for low-income children and families—and we both hoped to find a way to address their needs through our work. But Carol's real desire, she confessed, was to go back to school for her doctorate and become a social worker. I confided to her that I had always dreamed about starting my own school.

One of the things that had inspired me to join Parenting was an article I had read in a special issue of the magazine about African American boys. The story quoted a twelve-year-old boy from Chicago named Eric Boyd. "I wake up in the night and hear people shooting and noise from wild parties. I saw a teenager get shot in his head right in front of my building. My mother won't let me play outside because she's afraid they'll pressure me to be in a gang. She doesn't want me dead. I love math and reading. Some people from a company came and took us to visit engineers. I could be one! In the stories we read, wishes come true. But for the people I know, that never happens."

I'd torn out the page from the magazine with Eric's photo and quote, and put it in a black frame. Now, in my new office, I placed it on my desk next to a photo of my own children. Eric represented the reason why I was at Parenting, and, more fundamentally, why I had pursued my doctorate in education in the first place. I knew my job at the magazine wouldn't directly help this child, but I was hoping it would be a stepping-stone to helping others like him.

Soon Joel had come through the first round of chemo. The kids made "Welcome Home Daddy" signs and posted them in the family room. He still had to go to the hospital for checkups. But mostly—and miraculously—he was feeling better.

One Friday night after we'd put the kids to sleep, we were reading in bed when Joel told me to sit up and close my eyes. "What are you talking about?" I asked. "Just do it," he insisted. A minute later he put a smooth box in my hand. "Open it."

Inside was a beautiful necklace made of blue glass beads. He took my hands in his. "You saved my life," he said. "No, I didn't," I replied. "Yes. You did," he said, holding my hand tightly. I buried my head in his chest and silently prayed to God that he would stay healthy.

And he was. Slowly, he was building up stamina. He was determined to get better and he was stronger as each week passed.

Even while juggling my marketing and business development responsibilities at Parenting, I made it a priority to meet social entrepreneurs who were working to eradicate injustice. On a visit to Washington, D.C., I contacted Jonah Edelman, who had just started an organization called Stand for Children to train local communities to fight for children's best interests. Jonah's mother, Marian Wright Edelman, was a legendary civil rights activist and the founder of the Children's Defense Fund, a national organization that advocates for children. I had read several of her books and always revisited one line of hers that I had copied down in my journal: "Children need long distance, steady, persistent advocates who do the hard, quiet, thankless day-to-day work."

Jonah's office was a flurry of activity: Some fifteen young activists created brochures, others entered names into a database, and a small group sat in the corner planning an event. That evening, Jonah drove me to a community center where I observed him for several hours as he conducted a training session for parents on community organizing.

I was fired up. As soon as I got back to New York, I met with Carol and we immediately began brainstorming ideas that would use Parenting as a vehicle to support the needs of disenfranchised families. The one that excited me the most was a literacy project. Several newsmagazines had recently published cover stories about research on brain development from birth through age three. That research showed that early childhood education—specifically, parents reading books to preschoolers—was far more critical to brain development than experts had previously understood.

Parenting owned a distribution company that gave out goodie bags to all new mothers in the country through hospitals. These bags contained product samples, coupons, and literature. Our idea was to sell a series of books that were developmentally appropriate for each stage of the new baby's life. The new mother would get her first book free, then pay a fee each month for a new book that came at the right age. We could influence millions of mothers to read more to their young children just by getting that first book into their hands.

Brad was tasked with presenting the program's financial projections. "We ran the numbers and it looks good. As long as you cut out the municipal hospitals, this could be profitable." I looked around the room. Everyone was nodding. "But the municipal hospitals are the low-income families," I said. Brad looked at me incredulously. "Right, that's the point. They are the twenty-five percent of the market that can't afford fifty-nine dollars for a set of books."

"But those are the people who most need the books! They are the mothers who don't have access to the information about why it's so important to read to their infants. That's the whole point of the research—that's why we created this product," I said.

"Are you looking to ruin our margins? This is such a no-brainer," he argued. I pushed back: "Obviously we have to be profitable. But why can't we do some good as well. Why can't we find someone to sponsor the books for the lower-income mothers? Maybe Johnson & Johnson would do it. It's a great marketing opportunity for them. I'll sell it to J&J myself." One of the senior ad salesmen looked at Ellen, then stood up and looked at me. "J&J is my client. I have them locked in for an ad schedule and I don't want to distract them. We are not going to them with this proposal," he said.

Just at that moment, Michael walked by. Brad looked at me, rolled his eyes, stood up quickly and headed toward the door. "You got a minute?" he asked Michael, and the two of them walked away together.

I went back to my office, demoralized. What was I doing? More to the point, what was I doing *here*?

Carol poked her head in. "You okay?" she asked.

"Sure, I'll be fine. But I wish we could focus on our mission while also being profitable. You can do both, you know," I said, picking up our mission statement.

"Please," she said. "That's not our actual mission—it's marketing! The goal here is shareholder value for Time Warner. I think you're great, Deborah, but get real. There's no point . . ."

Ellen walked in. "Don't let me interrupt," she said.

"No, you're not interrupting, I was just leaving," Carol said, as she got up to leave.

Ellen stood in front of my desk and looked at the bookshelf behind me. It was filled with books about education, parenting, and a few about business.

"Why do you have so many books?" she asked. "It looks like a library in here, not an office."

I ignored the remark. "What's up?" I asked.

"Just wanted to make sure we're on the same page about J&J. Any new opportunities for them need to go through me. Have a great weekend."

It's not a mission, it's marketing. Carol's words rang in my ears. How could I have been so naïve? I thought it would be possible to achieve our revenue goals while also helping children by influencing new mothers. That was the whole reason I had been excited about this job. I couldn't care less about designing a new logo for the magazine.

I took out a notepad and wrote "School" on top. In the middle of the paper, I drew a stick figure—my best attempt at a child—then sketched out small circles all around the child, each circle connecting to the figure with a line. I wrote one word inside each circle: *love, books, values, confidence, nature, service, character, curiosity*. These were the things I thought a parent or teacher needed to focus on in order to raise a wholesome child.

Six months into the job, and I was not happy.

I met my friend Ilan for breakfast the next week. "I know that I'm lucky to have this job, but it's just not fulfilling. I feel like a misfit in this kind of corporate environment," I said. "I want to be part of something that is helping children or mothers." Ilan was a finance executive but he knew everyone, and was the type of person who was always eager to help others. "I have a friend at Sesame Street. They are much more mission oriented. You'd be happier there. I'll make a call."

The holidays were approaching. At work, Michael gathered the senior management team to give us each a gift. He had purchased Steuben glass animals, each representing his view of each person. He gave a bull to Ellen, a swan to the editor, and an owl to me. I didn't take it as a compliment.

A few days before New Year's, Michael called me into his office. "I'm sorry, Deborah, but I just don't think this is the right fit," he said. He was right. I suggested a slow transition that would benefit both of us. "How about I stay until late spring and finish up the projects I've been managing while I look for something else?" Michael agreed. "That sounds great," he said.

Great? I was thirty-six years old and unsuccessful at work. I did not have another job. And Joel wasn't yet out of the woods. This was anything but great.

Ilan's introduction to Sesame Street happened at the perfect time. They needed someone to lead their publishing division, which included *Sesame Street Parents* magazine, and I loved the idea of working for a company that prioritized underserved children. Sesame Street was ahead of the curve when it came to making learning fun and accessible for low-income preschoolers.

I started as the group publisher in the spring of 1999. The kids were doing well in school, and Joel was feeling even better. Of course, we had no guarantees about the future, and the fear of the cancer returning hovered over us. But it had been ten months and Joel was consistently improving. We were sure the worst was behind us. We were sure this would be a much better year.

I was looking forward to working at Sesame Street. The company's history inspired me. I particularly admired the late Jim Henson, creator of the Muppets, who had performed the characters of Ernie and Kermit. Prior to Sesame Street, Jim had spent many years working on commercials in order to support his dream. "It was a pleasure to get out of that world," he said before he died. I understood how he felt.

There was no question that I had been hired to bolster the commercial success of Sesame Street's publishing division. But what really excited me was the possibility of leveraging one of the world's most beloved brands for the greater good. I couldn't help but dream up ideas for how the magazine could go beyond the typical articles about family travel, food, and discipline, to provide more substantive advice for parents.

"Today's parents face enormous challenges," I wrote on a legal pad during those first days at work. "Powerful media messages insidiously influence our kids by glorifying materialism, focusing excessively on appearance, and promoting instant gratification." I looked at that page for a moment and thought to myself, this isn't a dissertation—simplify it! I crumpled it up and threw it in the trash. Then I wrote, "Provide parents with guidance on how to raise children of fine character who will make a contribution to society." I tore out the page and posted this vision on the bulletin board near my desk.

There was only one problem: It was not my place to be coming up with ideas like this at all. My job was to make the magazine profitable. So I tried to keep my mind on the business at hand.

I added regional sales offices, made some staffing changes, and developed promotional campaigns with Barnes & Noble, Kmart, and the new website eToys.com. For months I kept asking myself: how much longer until I can start doing something that matters?

Soon the trade publications began reporting dramatic improvements in Sesame Street's performance: we had increased sales, earnings, and market share. My team was thrilled with the success and we had a party to mark the good news.

Everyone was still celebrating when I went back to my office and stared at my vision statement, still pinned there on my bulletin board. Somehow the party had made me feel worse. There was nothing wrong with commercial success; I just didn't care about it.

I took out my notepad and wrote "Parent as Educator," then I looked up at the poster of Jim Henson on my wall. He had been with Sesame Street during its magical years. They did change the world in those days. I wished I could have been part of that.

As I sat in my office overlooking Lincoln Center, I felt trapped and frustrated.

What could I do? Who could I talk to?

Jonah Edelman of Stand for Children had told me about the chairman of his board, Geoffrey Canada, who ran a community organization in Harlem. I called him from my office phone that evening. "Hi, Geoffrey. I'm a friend of Jonah's. I hear wonderful things about your work. Could I stop by and learn more about what you're doing? Maybe there's a way I can be helpful?"

A few days later, I was sitting in Geoff's office in Harlem as he shared his plans to provide comprehensive services to low-income families. I made a donation on the spot, and later sent up a few boxes of Sesame Street toys. Geoff was inspiring, and I asked to see more of his organization in action. He told me about his new parent-training program. "Would it be possible to spend the day observing it?" I asked. "Sure, you can come by any weekend," he offered. I jumped at the chance.

That Saturday, I took the train into Harlem. I arrived early in the morning as pregnant women and new mothers with strollers showed up at the public school for workshops on child development and parenting.

I wanted to spend more time with those families, so I asked Geoff if there was some way I could get involved. He promised to keep me in mind.

Then, one morning in June as I was blow-drying my hair, Joel said he wasn't feeling well. "What's wrong?" I asked, still focused on my hair. "I just feel really bad," he said quietly. I switched off the blow-dryer and turned to him. "I think something is seriously wrong," he said.

By the end of the day, the threat of a relapse was no longer lurking in the shadows. The leukemia was back.

The painful treatments that Joel had bravely endured for a year had failed, and now the cancer was even more aggressive. His parents decided to immediately transfer him to MD Anderson, a premier cancer hospital in Houston.

The year before, Joel had told me that he could bear going through this once, but that his biggest fear was a relapse. He had worried that he wouldn't be able to make it through the chemo, the spinal taps, and the hospital a second time.

Thinking about it broke my heart.

I wanted to move to Houston so I could be with him. But how could I? The one thing our children needed more than anything was stability and routine. Still, I called Joel's doctor to discuss the possibility of moving to Houston.

"Maybe I can ask for some time off," I suggested. "They'll understand."

"No. They won't," the doctor replied bluntly. "You can't. It's not like you've worked there for ten years. You can't take a sabbatical. You just started."

Nearly two thousand miles from me, Joel lay in a hospital bed as a new set of oncologists put him through more tests. I flew to see him as often as possible. We were told that the only thing that would save him was a bone marrow transplant. Everyone in the family was tested for blood type, and the only match was his father, who had been by Joel's side all year.

After the surgery, the doctors explained that if Joel remained cancer-free for one hundred days, it would mean the procedure had been a success. They tested his blood daily, and he was kept in isolation to prevent any kind of infection.

Every night I'd rush in the door from work and run to the phone to call him. Another day down, closer every day, praying, a third of the way there . . .

Toward the end of the summer, I called him as usual. He picked up the phone. "Another good day?" I asked hopefully. But he could barely speak. The test results were bad. The procedure—our last hope—had failed. I immediately booked the next flight to Houston.

Joel's eyes lit up when I walked into the room the next day. I walked toward him, smiling, holding back my tears, as I'd become accustomed to doing every day at work and around the kids. "Come lie down with me," he said quietly.

I got into the hospital bed with him. As we rested there together, I promised Joel that things would get better. They would find another treatment. I refused to see reality. I refused to let him see reality. There is no way to describe the pain of watching someone you love slowly dying.

Joel's doctors told me and his parents about an experimental drug. It was very strong and it had not yet been approved. Would we support its use for Joel? The potential side effects could include death. There were three people on whom it had been tested and one was still alive. But it was the only chance. His family and I agreed. We had no other choice. Now all we could do was wait and hope.

For months, I shuttled between work in the city, the children at home, and Joel in the hospital in Houston. And I prayed for a miracle.

Not that it mattered, but things were going very well at work. My boss had announced that she was leaving Sesame Street. She had been offered a fantastic new job as head of the magazine trade association. They'd decided to promote me to group president.

Every morning, I'd cry in the shower, get the kids off to school, and cry in the car to and from the office. But at the office, I put on a professional face. Nobody was really aware of what I was going through.

Before we knew it, Thanksgiving was around the corner. The whole family gathered in Houston to be with Joel for the holiday. The kids—now eleven, nine, and eight—his parents, his brothers and sister, and I all shared a small rented apartment near the hospital. The experimental drug made things worse; every day Joel's health was deteriorating before our eyes.

Then one day in late December, the doctor called to tell me to come back right away. Joel had been rushed to intensive care.

It was the middle of the night when I walked into the ICU. It was silent and completely dark, just blinking lights and the soft humming of machines. The doctor walked over and stood silently for a moment. "I am sorry to have to tell you this," he said, "but there is nothing more we can do to save your husband."

There was an agonizing decision to make. Do I stay by his side in the final hours? Or do I fly home now to be with the children at that awful moment? It tore me apart, but everyone agreed the right thing was for me to be with the children.

When the doctor left the room I could barely stand. I held Joel's hand, kissed his forehead, and whispered, "I love you," tears streaming down my face. The only thought running through my head was, I wish it were me instead of you. I wish it were me.

The next day was December 23, and the children were home for the holiday break. I knew my life was about to end the moment the phone rang. When the call finally came, I didn't want to answer it. Somehow—I don't know how—I forced my hand to pick it up. There was a long moment of silence. Time stood still. Then I heard the words I had been dreading for eighteen months. "He's gone," my brother-in-law said, choking back tears.

In an instant, the world stopped. Our house felt like a body without a soul.

I gathered the kids together, holding them all to me. I froze. This can't really be happening. What should I do? How can I tell them?

"Daddy has died." I said the words, and looked at the sad, confused faces of my three children. I held them all close. "Daddy loved you more than anything in the world. He is looking down from heaven and he still loves you. And I love you. And all your grandparents and aunts and uncles love you. Everything is going to be okay."

I didn't actually believe that. I didn't think anything would ever be okay. I was certain my life was now over.

The entire family was gathering at my in-laws' home in McLean, Virginia, where Joel and his four siblings had grown up. That night my brothers-in-law kept a fire going in the fireplace as we wrote our eulogies, tossing drafts into the fire, crying while we wrote, tossing tissues into the fire, talking about how impossible it would be to capture Joel's life in a speech.

Just a few hours later, we woke up and it was time to go to the funeral. When we walked into the room, I was taken aback when I saw the casket. Then I looked at our children, so innocent and heartbroken. I still could not believe what was happening.

We took our seats and Joel's older brother spoke first. "He wanted to understand the universe," David said. "But he wouldn't hesitate to cheat you at poker just to see if you were paying attention." Dan said, "It didn't matter what you were doing, when Joel walked into the room, you knew it was going to get better—and it always did, cracking everyone up the way only he could." Jon talked about how Joel was his role model. His sister Sarah spoke directly to our children: "Your dad's love for you is the very strongest kind of love that exists. He tried so incredibly hard to stay here with us."

I was last. I could barely breathe. I could barely stand. But I felt that I had to do it. Slowly, I walked to the podium. I was afraid to start speaking. Everyone waited and looked on, and I did not look up. Somehow, finally I uttered the words I'd written the night before:

"A tribute to Joel's life seems an impossible task. Joel was larger than life. He was one of those very rare individuals born to a higher purpose, and put to higher tests. There are simply no words that will ever do justice . . ." Then I went on to try to describe his extraordinary intellect, kindness, humility, and creative genius.

At the end of the ceremony, we played "Angel" by Jimi Hendrix. Joel had loved Hendrix, and we always thought he was a little bit like him.

When we arrived at the grave site, I thought: this does not make any sense, this is for old people. It was surreal to see the casket lowered into the ground, surreal to stand with our three children, guiding them in reciting the traditional prayer for mourning. For a year after this day, I would take them to synagogue every Sabbath so they could recite the mourner's prayer and, I hoped, connect with their father and find solace through the congregation.

After the burial, someone, I don't remember who, told me to go into the car. I walked through the muddy grass in my black knit dress and black high heels, holding hands with the kids. When I looked out the back window of the car, I saw my religious cousins personally filling the grave with dirt and saying prayers. I wanted to escape from the car. I pictured myself running back to the pile of dirt and throwing myself on the ground.

I don't remember how we got back to the house, but every room was overflowing with people. My mind was a fog. I walked into the kitchen, where Joel's father was standing by the counter.

"What are we supposed to do now?" I asked Bob.

"I was just thinking the same thing," he said.

When we returned to our house in Westchester the next day, my cousins had already let themselves in and made lasagna for dinner. As the week went by, friends, teachers, old boyfriends, family members—the whole world, it seemed—showed up for shiva, the seven days of Jewish mourning. My camp friends flew in from around the country. We talked about Joel all day and prayed at night. The prayers were like a rhythm.

On the third night, the police showed up. There were so many cars and so many people in the neighborhood that they wanted to see if everything was okay.

My sister Alisa—eight months pregnant with her first child—coordinated all communications with friends and family. My mother, so devoted to her grandchildren, took care of them and cooked us meals. My father and uncle tried to help by fixing things, like the screen that had completely fallen off the door leading out to the deck, the girls' bedroom door that wouldn't close, the leaky faucet in the kitchen. Joel had been quite handy and could fix anything, but in the eighteen months when he was sick, much of the house had fallen apart. "You need to maintain your home," they said, "or the small problems will become bigger problems later." I heard but did not really hear. All I remember saying is, "If it's not a person, I just can't think about it right now."

The first days of 2000 were surreal. The kids and I were supposed to go back to "normal" life. I knew that the most nurturing thing for children is to maintain routines so I wanted to get them back to school. There had been no time for shopping, so breakfast was Cheerios and milk. I didn't allow myself to feel anything; I just focused on the kids and my job as a mother. We can function, we can move forward with our day, you will go to school. So I went outside with them, smiling and waving good-bye. After the bus drove away, all our neighbors surrounded me, and told me again how sorry they were. I thanked them as they looked at me sympathetically. Then I went back to the house.

I walked through the door and went straight upstairs to the bedroom. It was the first moment I had been alone since Joel had died. I started gasping for air as I was having trouble breathing. My head started spinning and I felt dizzy. Then I suddenly collapsed on the floor sobbing, and called out his name over and over. I cried for what seemed like hours. I could not lift my body off the floor. I did not know how to go on with my life.

Even though shiva was over, person after person called or came over, still trying to make me feel better. Often they'd give me books on recovery and grieving. I hated the word *grief*; I thought it was self-centered. I was touched that everyone wanted to help, but they didn't understand that I didn't care about feeling better. I did not open one of those books. The only thing I wanted was to be able to switch places with Joel, to give him back his life. So unless one of those books could make that switch happen, I wasn't interested.

I made a point of talking about Joel constantly so the kids would remember him—praising him frequently but also passing along little things, like what kinds of vegetables he liked. Our eight-year-old, Rachel, came home from school and showed me a poem she had written in her third-grade classroom about Joel. "How will I live without him? Life was so fun, but now it's so dim." I thought Rachel captured exactly how we all felt.

And in his fifth-grade class, Avi was working on a time capsule. The teacher had asked each student to have both of their parents write them a letter that they would open in a few years, when they graduated from eight grade.

I wrote to him: "Son, whatever you do in life, remember that happiness lies in living a life based on eternal values, such as integrity, service and compassion. Dad set a wonderful example for you. But this doesn't just happen. You have to make it happen in your life. And it's harder than it seems. Most of the media will give you the false sense that happiness can be found through wealth, prestige, or beauty. But those things are shallow and empty. None satisfy the soul."

I thought about the fact that in a few years, when he opened the letter at the end of eighth grade, he would be reading only one letter when his friends would be reading two letters. So I added, "Dad and I are very proud of you. I say 'are' because even though Dad isn't with us here in the physical world, he is watching over you in spirit."

Each morning I didn't think I could make it through the day, and then somehow I did. At one point I thought the only way the pain would ever stop would be if I were to also die, even though I never considered suicide as an option. Doctors and friends suggested that I take some medication to dull the pain, but I didn't believe in drugs. So I tried running. It helped just a little. But as I ran each morning, the same thought consumed me: I want Joel back.

The main thing that helped was talking with Joel's brothers on the phone every night. Dan and Jon would tell me stories about Joel from childhood and I'd tell them stories from the last twelve years. Somehow talking about Joel with his brothers who missed him and loved him as much as I did got me through those dark weeks.

I couldn't sleep so I would read for hours late into the night, until I could no longer keep my eyes open. On weekends, I took the kids to the library or bookstore, and I picked up a few books for myself each time. I usually browsed the education and business sections. The first books that interested me were by Jonathan Kozol: *Amazing Grace* and *Savage Inequalities*. They were all about children living in poverty in America. I knew that public schools in poor neighborhoods were bad, but Kozol brought them to life with devastating, vivid detail. The children profiled in his books were aware of the inequality—"they give us the very worst schools anyone could think of," one young girl said in *Amazing Grace*—and talked about how they felt trapped in failing schools in unsafe neighborhoods.

Once I started reading Kozol's books, I could not put them down.

There were so many tragic stories. But the one that really got to me was in *Savage Inequalities*. A boy named Christopher from East St. Louis told Kozol he thought Martin Luther King had died in vain. "You asked a question about Martin Luther King," Christopher said to Kozol. "I'm going to say something. All that stuff about 'the dream' means nothing to the kids I know . . . he died in vain. He was famous and he lived and gave his speeches and he died and now he's gone. But we're still here. Don't tell students in this school about 'the dream.'" That was the saddest thing I'd ever heard a child say. Though he'd grown up in the richest country on earth, he had lost all hope at such a young age.

Christopher and the other children made me think about my own children. I was a young mother, suddenly alone, reading about young mothers, many also alone. I felt connected to them.

The difference, of course, was that I had been blessed with privileges, like a good education, simply by accident of birth. My education gave me opportunities that enabled me to provide the same opportunities for my children. Joel and I had the choice to purchase a home in a neighborhood with good schools. This ensured that our children would have a quality education. The families in Kozol's books wanted the same for their children. Why shouldn't they have the same choice I had? It did not seem fair. It was not right.

It had been months, and everyone kept telling me that "time will heal," but it wasn't. Then on another sleepless night I opened Viktor Frankl's classic, *Man's Search for Meaning*. Frankl was a psychiatrist in the Nazi concentration camps who studied the connection between physical suffering and mental outlook. "We needed to stop asking about the meaning of life," he wrote, "and instead to think of ourselves as those who were being questioned by life. We had to teach the despairing men that it did not really matter what we expected from life, but rather what life expected from us."

What did life expect? That question helped me. It spoke to me more than anything I'd read or heard since Joel had died. For so long, my friends wanted to make me feel better, but I just didn't care about feeling better. Frankl's question appealed to something deeper, to an inner sense of responsibility.

As I read, I decided that life expected me to get over my own pain, and to do something for those who were suffering more. I wanted to help Christopher and other children like those in Kozol's books. And I began to feel certain that life expected me to. I wanted to be part of the solution, as my camp counselors used to say. But what would I do?

The first call I made was to the director of the battered women's clinic where we had donated the extra food after the shiva ended. I visited her in Yonkers, and she talked with conviction about the importance of their work. The next week I went to see Dr. James Comer at the Yale Child Study Center. The week after that I met with Dr. Vincent Fontana, who pioneered child abuse prevention at the New York Foundling Hospital. Then I went to Washington, D.C., to meet with Lee Schorr, author of two books that had captivated me: *Within Our Reach* and *Common Purpose*.

The following month I visited a homeless shelter in Times Square, and a food bank in the Bronx. I met wonderful women who were raising children while trying to overcome tremendous economic hardship, escape abusive partners, or battle drug addiction. These mothers wanted the same things for their children that I wanted for mine. They were just handed a harder lot in life.

On the weekends, I continued to go with my kids to Barnes & Noble or the library. I picked up books on education, business, and child development. I stayed up night after night until two-thirty or three in the morning reading about social entrepreneurs who were dedicating their lives to ameliorating society's most intractable problems.

"What did life expect?" Frankl had asked. I had been thinking about this for a while. And now I asked myself, What did life expect of me, specifically?

As I thought about the individuals in these books, the places I had visited and the people I had met, one issue struck me as different from all the others: education.

Education was different because it was the only thing that could be the underlying solution to virtually all the other pathologies I'd read about and seen firsthand. Without education, as the children in Kozol's books had felt, there was no hope. Without education, then a child like Christopher would come to ask if Dr. King had died in vain.

If I cared about social justice, then I would have to put my sadness aside, and start doing something to help children like Christopher.

CHAPTER 3

PEOPLE, NOT PRODUCT

I STARTED TO WAKE UP EACH day thinking about Christopher and the millions of children just like him who were trapped in failing schools. I wondered about Christopher's mother. Was she frustrated every single morning as she sent him off to a failing school, wishing she could do more for him? Why couldn't something be done for all these children?

Why were America's schools failing on such a massive scale? There was not a single urban school district in America where all children were learning at grade level—not one.

There were a handful of great public schools in every city, like Frederick Douglass Academy in Harlem. The problem was that such schools were the rare exception.

What could be done to fix this? The country did not need someone to open another great school, I concluded. What was needed was a radical transformation of the entire public school system.

In 1992, media entrepreneur Chris Whittle had founded the

Edison Project in an attempt to do just that. Edison, a for-profit company that managed schools, was controversial from the moment it was founded. Whittle was offering a direct challenge to the government-funded monopoly of public schools.

I was curious about the project, so I visited Edison's headquarters in midtown Manhattan. It was after 6 p.m., but the offices were still packed with people and buzzing with energy. Chris greeted me and introduced me to Benno Schmidt. Remarkably, Chris had persuaded Benno to leave his position as president of Yale University to join Edison as chairman.

By 2000 Edison was the largest private operator of public schools in the country, with more than one hundred schools in twenty-one states. Their size and success made the potential for large-scale reform seem possible. Chris's pitch was filled with private-sector analogies—"FedEx has a ninety-nine percent delivery rate, yet only twenty-nine percent of children in high-poverty communities are reading at grade level," he said—and he talked about investing in R&D and pushing for educational innovation.

Chris said that Edison contracted with public school districts and boards to run two kinds of public schools: contract and charter. I was curious to understand the difference. Contract schools, he explained, were traditional public schools that hired a for-profit company to manage them. The teachers in contract schools remained unionized, though, so I didn't see how such a model could change the system.

Then he told me about charter schools.

The first charter school law had passed in Minnesota in 1991. Charter schools were public schools that were given freedom from union rules in exchange for being held accountable to produce results. If they failed to achieve their academic goals, the state could take away the charter and shut down the school. No red tape, no bureaucracy. Just entrepreneurial spirit, freedom, and accountability.

The instant Chris described charter schools, I was drawn to the idea. It was the one thing I had come across that I thought had the potential to actually change the education system. And that, after all, was precisely what I was passionate about: changing the system itself. As I sat there listening to him tell me about the charter movement, I felt that I had found my calling.

"Are there any charter schools in New York City?" I asked him. Yes, a few had just opened.

Chris was very clear: this new movement was small now, but it was about to change American public education forever.

Then he made me a job offer.

It took a minute to register. I'd met Chris not an hour ago, and now he was outlining what my responsibilities might be.

I absolutely loved the charter school concept, but I was hesitant about the fact that Edison was a for-profit enterprise running schools, even if they did report to a public entity.

Many opposed Edison on principle, but Chris argued that the company's private-sector status allowed them the flexibility to provide a better education for students—and ultimately, he argued compellingly, that's what should matter. Besides, textbook publishers, school bus companies, and food service providers earned profits from schools every day.

Chris had assembled an impressive team of respected educators. Like Edison himself, Chris was a pioneer. His vision was sweeping. He had a grand plan for system-wide change. And he urged me to be a part of it.

Here was an opportunity to work with driven people, learn about education reform, and hopefully contribute to improving schools while earning a paycheck. The rest, I'd figure out later.

My first assignment at Edison was to help a new team that had just formed to secure contracts for four schools in New York City. Little did I know that this would be my introductory course in union politics.

Mayor Rudy Giuliani had announced that he would invite proposals from private-school operators in early 2001 to manage ten of the city's worst public schools. The mayor was sure that the school management companies, which offered a longer school day, tutoring, and a succeed-or-shut-down sense of urgency, could improve these chronically failing schools. The teachers' union was livid with Giuliani's proposal.

Edison's chief operating officer, Chris Cerf, was in charge of negotiating with the union. "The union is exceptionally shrewd," he explained to me. "They have a savvy political machine and the best PR minds in the country. They get up every morning thinking about how to kill off the charter movement. That's what they do every day: work full-time to protect adults. Even if the laws ruin the lives of God knows how many children."

"They're ruthless," an Edison principal based in Maryland told me. "They pay groups to come out and protest as if they represent local parents in the community." I couldn't believe that, but I would soon see it for myself. New York City had more than one thousand schools, and I wondered why the union would spend so much time and money fighting against the creation of just a few good schools.

I observed the whole process from the inside, and it was quite a spectacle. I tagged along with the Edison team whenever possible. I stood in the back of the room as they attended a press conference at Al Sharpton's Harlem headquarters where he announced his opposition to Edison. I listened to Chris Cerf speak with reporters who told him the union had arranged thousands of robo-calls to mislead parents into believing the Edison-managed public schools would be charging tuition. I watched from a third-floor classroom window as unionized teachers from a failing school held up "Parents Say No to Edison" protest signs, only to go inside the school to start working after the local NBC and ABC camera trucks left. The union was so shrewd, so powerful, and so well organized that it was relatively easy for them to crush the mayor's project.

I had always believed in unions. Most of my summer camp counselors were liberal, some were socialists. We all supported better treatment of workers and the disenfranchised.

Growing up immersed in these values, it never occurred to me that this ideology could result in the poor treatment of low-income children. Yet in just a matter of months, I had become completely disillusioned by union politics.

In her book *Nothing's Impossible*, the founder of Frederick Douglass Academy, Lorraine Monroe, explained, "The teacher's union would be a major headache for anyone in the principal's role. They'd filed almost a hundred grievances in the previous year, tying the principal up with hearings." Meanwhile, she added, "kids were running up and down the halls and playing their boom boxes during class." The union did not allow principals like Lorraine Monroe to hire the teachers she wanted or to fire incompetent teachers.

Then there was tenure. After only two years in the classroom, teachers had guaranteed jobs for life regardless of their performance. Teachers who had "breathed the longest," as education reformers liked to say, got to keep their jobs, regardless of the academic success of their students. Teacher compensation was based solely on seniority, with no connection to quality or student learning outcomes.

I learned from Chris that the union spent millions of dollars to influence political leaders and to litigate against principals who wanted to fire ineffective teachers, all in the name of "due process" and fairness. (What about fairness for the children, I wondered.) If a motivated teacher wanted to stay late and tutor a student on his own time, well, too bad. Union rules would not allow it.

I heard time after time from teachers who had been scolded by union reps for staying after three o'clock to tutor a student. This extra effort was "setting a bad example." Other teachers told me stories of holding secret study groups with a few colleagues in coffee shops, for fear of being "caught" putting in extra time to improve their practice.

All of these rules added up to a school system completely devoid of adult accountability. It was a system that made it impossible for schools to function and allowed children's lives to be wasted. It was a moral outrage, and the people at Edison were intent on doing something about it.

To launch Edison, Chris had gathered some of the best minds in the country to develop a "school design." For two years, they had culled through the latest research, examined curricula, and deliberated about which programs were most effective. Once they gathered all that data, they crafted Edison's design.

Edison's brochures described their lofty ideals—"Liberty and the conviction that learning is the surest path to individual opportunity and social progress"—and their ambitious plans like cutting-edge technology and personalized instruction.

It all sounded amazing. And in theory, it was. The founding team had addressed every single detail of the school's design. What that meant, however, was that every aspect of the school was predetermined: the curriculum, student-teacher ratio, textbooks, daily schedule, staffing structure—everything.

Like others that came before and after Edison, they often used the terms "research-based" and "proven" when talking about their school design. It may be "proven," I thought to myself, but that doesn't mean anything if the individual teacher does not own it. It was the design team that owned it. They had made all the decisions. As much as they tried to communicate their plans down to teachers through training, still it was *their* design.

This top-down approach directly conflicted with something that I believed was critically important: teacher empowerment. Many education reformers also said they believed in empowerment. But I was coming to realize that most often they intended it to be for schools and school principals, not necessarily for teachers.

Over the course of many months, I asked the Edison education team a lot of questions and accepted every invitation they offered to visit their schools and attend their training conferences. The schools run by Edison definitely seemed better. They reported that their test scores had increased four points per year on average. But as I observed classes and spoke with teachers and principals, I began to see a gap between their theoretical school design and the day-to-day reality on the ground.

For example, the school design team had selected "Success for All," a highly prescribed literacy program that dictates exactly what a teacher should say and do for the entire lesson. After I had logged many hours sitting in the back of classrooms, I started asking the teachers what they thought of it. Some of them loved it. Others couldn't stand it.

"It's frustrating," said a bright young woman who had been recruited to teach at Edison after three years' experience in a Philadelphia district school. "I can't stand following a script. There are so many times every morning when I hear a child read incorrectly and I know what I should be saying and doing to help him learn. But we are not allowed to go off script."

I asked two other teachers who had just finished their Success for All lesson for the day, and they got into a heated debate. "It prevents me from teaching at a higher level," said a veteran reading teacher. His colleague disagreed. "Hey, at least we don't have to spend any time planning lessons." she said.

When I asked the academic director her opinion of the program, she spoke in a hushed tone. "It's teacher-proof," she told me. "Teacher-proof?" I asked. "Yes. It's scripted. So it works even with the crappy teachers we can't fire."

The same thing happened when I talked to teachers about other aspects of the school. Some teachers loved the math program; others couldn't stand it. Some thought Wilson Reading was effective for reading remediation; others had been trained in different programs they thought would be better. But what they all had in common was a lack of empowerment. They had not been allowed to make the decisions about how to teach.

It wasn't just Edison. The more I studied and talked with education reformers, the more it became clear that teachers were so often told what to do—whether they taught in district schools, charter schools, or Edison schools. Each year, they were trained in the latest fad or "comprehensive reform" that someone else had created. They were cogs in the machine.

I disagreed with this "school design" approach. It's not that there was anything wrong with Edison's design. But the very concept of a school design—a program created by a few experts to be replicated by teachers—was never going to work. It was top-down.

I wrote in my journal, "Revolutions need to be bottom-up."

It seemed so clear to me that replication would not fix public education—yet somehow, education research still focused on how to replicate the common elements of excellent schools. They spoke in platitudes like "Excellent schools have high expectations, strong leaders, and quality instruction . . ." Blah, blah, blah.

It reminded me of those Sunday Night Football commentators that Joel used to make fun of. He called them masters of the obvious. "If they want to win this game, they're going to need to throw the football and make some completions," Joel would say in a mock announcer's voice.

Most education scholars pointed to specific aspects of the educational program as being most essential: smaller class size, a particular approach to teaching reading, a particular way of scheduling classes. They all focused on how to fix the educational program—the product.

The book that articulated my gut feelings about the importance of empowering teachers—and the book that would prove the most pivotal in my thinking about the nation's education system—was *Management Challenges for the 21st Century*, by the renowned management guru Peter Drucker. His basic premise was that the conditions required for productivity in the twentieth-century industrial economy, which revolved around manual workers, were completely different from the conditions required for productivity in the twenty-first-century knowledge economy, which revolved around knowledge workers.

Manual worker productivity, explained Drucker, requires that the manager tell the workers exactly how to do their jobs, but knowledge worker productivity requires that the manager provide workers with clear goals and autonomy. Drucker argued that knowledge worker productivity was more about the *attitude* of the knowledge worker.

I thought about how his idea could be applied to the education system. For one thing, it occurred to me that teachers are the consummate knowledge workers, yet they were being treated like manual workers.

For me, Drucker's most penetrating insight was that workers who are told exactly what to do stay incompetent. They become passive and apathetic because they have no ownership. This was exactly the problem in public schools. I thought we had to stop telling teachers exactly what to do. We needed to elevate them to their rightful position as knowledge workers.

Drucker also wrote about *kaizen*, the Japanese concept of workers continually improving the organization. It seemed to me that the idea of kaizen would be just as important for schools.

While I hadn't met anyone in the education sector who had implemented Drucker's approach, I was sure there had to be business leaders who had followed his ideas. After a bit of research, I came across an article in *BusinessWeek* about David Kearns.

David had been CEO of Xerox for almost a decade when President George H. W. Bush asked him to serve as U.S. deputy secretary of education in 1991. He had steered Xerox back from the brink of bankruptcy, and he was one of the earliest business leaders to champion national education reform.

I decided to track him down, first by cold calling the main number at Xerox. I had no idea if he would be there, since he had retired. But David was still there, and he took my call. We talked about our mutual fascination with the Japanese approach to business and education. When I told him that I was interested in learning about education reform, he invited me to meet with him at the Xerox corporate headquarters in Stamford, Connecticut.

At a conference table in his office, David told me about his efforts to fix the nation's education system in the early 1990s, how he and colleagues in the Bush administration had formed a public-private partnership with governors, CEOs, and scholars, and invested over a hundred million dollars into researching excellent schools and effective curricula. They packaged their various school designs like products—even giving them names and logos. They conducted presentations to pitch their designs in the hopes of getting teachers, principals, and superintendents to "buy in"—just like marketing a product. To support the implementation of their school designs, they created training programs and extensive support systems. Their goal was to fix education in America by convincing schools to replicate these designs. That replication approach was basically what Edison had done.

In the end, after disseminating all the best practices reinforced by quality control systems, after all that time, money, and effort, Kearns told me candidly, he and his fellow reformers had been unable to achieve their ambitious goals of dramatic transformation of the school system. Some incremental changes had taken place, but the bottom line was that children were still trapped in failing schools. The system as it had always functioned remained intact.

As I walked out of his office, I thought about the story he had told me. I got in my car and started driving out of the Xerox parking lot. Kearns had galvanized the country's most powerful political and business leaders and the brightest minds in education research. They were talented, driven, and well funded. Yet the nation's educational performance had not improved.

Why?

They had approached education as a product that could be replicated—and they had treated teachers like manual workers instead of knowledge workers.

I pulled over to the shoulder on I-95 and stopped the car. I took out my notebook and wrote: "Education is not about developing products. It's about developing people."

CHAPTER 4

PROVIDENCE

TEACHERS WERE THE ANSWER. Though I hadn't worked out the details, I was sure the only way to fix education was to focus on people—the teachers—to cultivate their passion and tap into their talent.

The question was *how*.

How to give every child in America an excellent teacher? I would be obsessed by this question for the next ten years.

I'd been thinking about how to change the system, how to eradicate educational inequity. I'd read dozens of books, met with experts, and learned a lot from listening to teachers. Finally I'd developed at least a basic strategy: Instead of creating the ideal school design as a product to be replicated by teachers, we needed to design schools *for* teachers, schools that would support teachers, and enable them to do their best work and bring out their highest potential.

But I wouldn't accomplish anything by just thinking and talking and reading. I had to *do it*—to get into the trenches and challenge the current system by starting a school system of my own.

That was my dream.

The reality was that my "people, not product" strategy wouldn't pay the bills. Joel hadn't had life insurance—who thinks of these things when you're young? All I had was a small savings account. It could sustain me and my three children for about six months, but it was for emergency use only. I was never supposed to touch it.

So I had no real plan and barely any money. The one thing I did have was a firm sense of commitment. I was committed for the sake of Christopher, stuck in the failing school in East St. Louis; I was committed for Eric Boyd, trapped in the housing project in Chicago. And I was committed for the mothers and children I had met in Yonkers, the South Bronx, and Harlem.

Back in my first month of college, I'd copied down a quote in my journal about commitment and providence. I had read it many times. So I opened my journal now to reread it again:

> The moment one definitely commits oneself, then
> Providence moves too. All sorts of things occur to help one
> that would never otherwise have occurred. A whole stream
> of events issues from the decision, raising in one's favor all
> manner of unforeseen incidents and meetings and material
> assistance, which no man could have dreamed would have
> come his way. Whatever you can do, or dream you can do,
> begin it. Boldness has genius, power, and magic in it.

Commitment. *Providence*. This was it. I would use my savings to start a system of schools, to work on the front lines of reform. Somehow I'd figure it out. I was all in.

I called my friend Sharon to tell her that I was leaving Edison to start schools in Harlem with my emergency savings. "We need to talk," she said. "I'm calling everyone. Meet us at California Pizza Kitchen at eight."

We'd barely sat down when Sharon spoke up. "Look," she said, "one thing you've never been is normal." Everyone laughed, but she hushed them. "Seriously. What are you going to do when you run out of money? I mean, we love you, but you're not thinking clearly. It's not the right time in your life. You have no security."

"What's the worst that could happen?" I said. "If I fail and run out of money, I'll just pitch a tent in my parents' backyard!"

"You can joke about it," Jeff said, "but what will happen when you *do* run out of money? You have a mortgage. Didn't it take you ten years to pay off your student loans? Aren't you afraid you could lose your house?"

"The only thing that scares me," I told them, "is how depressed I will be if I don't do this."

The food arrived, but nobody paid attention. They were all staring at me. "Do you even have any idea what you're doing or how to go about doing it?"

"No," I admitted, "but I have to try."

"So how about starting slowly," Sharon suggested. "You could volunteer at that new mothers' training program you visited in Harlem."

"And what about your wardrobe, your vacations, the kids' music lessons? I mean, everything is going to be different. Why do you always have to be so damn radical? Are you seriously ready to change your lifestyle?" asked Jeff.

"Actually I've thought about that already," I said. "There are about seven or eight things I have to give up and I'm willing to do it. I've made a list, and—"

"Of course she has," interrupted Becky, as everyone laughed.

And on it went. By the time dessert arrived, everyone had agreed my plan was a bad idea. While the others were devouring the brownies and ice cream, Larry sat silently, drinking his coffee. Finally he said, "It's noble that you want to use your life to serve others. We just want you to be realistic."

But they didn't get it. I wasn't being noble. I *had* to do this. I felt like I would die if I didn't.

The next morning was back to reality. Up at 6 a.m. to make breakfast, sign permission slips, put school lunches into backpacks, and get Avi, Rachel, and Chava onto the school bus.

Once the kids were out the door, I decided to set up an office to convince myself that my idea was more than a pipe dream. I cleared away board games, tennis racquets, and other equipment from the corner of a small playroom in our basement. I dragged over a light gray laminated desk I had bought the prior year for twenty-two dollars at a garage sale. I added a navy blue chair, a flimsy bookshelf, a file cabinet, and a computer and printer. Then I called Verizon to schedule installation of a phone line in the basement. (Those were the days of dial-up AOL.) My work attire was sweatpants and an old T-shirt.

I sat down at the desk and took out a notepad. On top I wrote "School Startup." Then I underlined it. Twice.

How do you start something from nothing? I asked myself as my mind wandered. I found myself staring at the rust on the filing cabinet. Then I became distracted by listening intently to lawn mowers outside the basement window. Time to relocate.

Our family room had always been my favorite. The walls were lined with bookshelves, and the large windows had a view of the woods in the backyard. I thought about Joel, but then forced the thought out of my head. I couldn't allow myself to fall backward into sorrow.

Okay, just *think*, I told myself. What should be my first step? I wrote the number 1 and circled it. I wanted to write out a long list but I couldn't come up with anything. So I put down the notepad on the coffee table, and went into the kitchen to make some tea.

Ten minutes later I was back on the couch and back to the notepad, steaming mug in hand. I picked up my pen and made a box around the words "school startup." I made a second box around the words. I drew a little stick figure on the top right corner of the paper. Then I labeled him Christopher, and gave him five little stick figure friends.

I looked out the window, then at a painting Joel had made for me while he was in the hospital, and then back at the lined paper. I looked at the pile I had gathered on the coffee table. There were lots of papers and books, and notepads filled with my ideas. I had a strategy: people, not product. Why couldn't I get moving?

I had no idea how to begin. What I needed was an actionable task list. But I didn't really know what I was doing. Was this even possible? Maybe my friends were right. Maybe this whole thing was as ridiculous as it sounded. I was lonely and I missed Joel.

The kids would be home from school in two hours and my approach was clearly going nowhere. So I put down the empty pad, laced up my sneakers, and went out to run.

As I was running, I gave myself a Nike-inspired pep talk: Just Do It. Don't look back. Keep moving forward. I told myself to figure out the two or three top priorities and focus on them like a laser. I pounded the pavement. Halfway up a killer hill, it hit me: funding. Seed money was the most important thing I'd need to begin. Without it, nothing would get off the ground. The second priority would be applying for charters. No money, no charters equals no schools. It had taken me half a day to realize the incredibly obvious.

I sprinted for the last minute to the house, pushed the door open, threw off my sneakers, and ran into the family room. I grabbed the pad and pen, ran downstairs to my new office, and sat at the desk. I tore off the first page and started fresh. On the top of one page I wrote "Funding" and on top of a second I wrote "Charters."

Starting even one charter school was a massive undertaking. There would be literally hundreds of things I'd need in place to get approval.

But very little information was available. It could take days or even weeks of research to piece together even basic facts for each question in the application.

In 2001, the New York State charter movement was in its infancy. In New York City, only a handful of charter schools existed, and most had not been operating long enough to have a track record.

I tried to develop a startup task list, but I didn't really know what to do. So instead I created categories—academics, teacher recruiting, parents and community involvement, compliance and policies, operations and finance, governance, and facilities. Unfortunately, there was not much I could apply from my experience at Edison; they had a corporate infrastructure, so their checklists had tasks like "coordinate with recruiting department." Plus, they had no schools in New York.

Finally, there was the issue of funding. Getting the charter sounded like it might be difficult, but securing the seed funding felt next to impossible. I had no experience with fundraising and no clue where to go or whom to approach.

By the time the school would eventually open, my list would grow to over 740 tasks. For now, I had only a few dozen items. I was figuring out from scratch what needed to be on the list while executing on the tasks each day. It was like trying to build a boat while rowing it.

What I really needed was a team. But I couldn't hire anyone because I couldn't afford to pay anyone a salary. So I decided to look for educational conferences, hoping that might be a way to meet potential funders or influential leaders who might know funders. I was excited to come across a conference called Education Leaders Council, which would be held in September in Atlanta. I didn't know anything about the group, but it sounded interesting and it was my first real lead. I registered immediately.

The conference would be in three months. That would be the halfway point to running out of my savings. Money was a huge stress, but there were others. For one, I was concerned about being taken seriously at such a conference. I was a young, single mother with an idea—that's it. I didn't even have a business card.

On that score, my friend Harriet saved the day. She ran a small public relations firm on Madison Avenue and I asked her if I could use her office address on the business cards of my nonexistent entity. "I can't use my home address," I explained. "That would be lame."

"Of course, darling!" she offered. I set up a Web domain and an email address, and went to Kinko's to print business cards and stationery with the address she loaned me.

Each day, I continued working methodically through the tasks. I met with a legal aid organization to set up nonprofit status. I drove to the local branch of Chase, where a bank officer helped me set up an account. When I told my father what I was up to, he generously volunteered to provide the first two thousand dollars so that I could attend the Atlanta conference. I set up a filing system and started reading and organizing materials. And I kept scribbling little notes about my strategy: "Teachers are the center of our universe. Nothing is more important."

Each day, I'd get the kids off to school, work all day, spend a few hours with them eating dinner and doing homework, then work again after they went to bed, usually until midnight. On weekends I'd take them to synagogue, then we'd change clothes and it was off to ballet and karate, then back home to change clothes again for baseball or soccer. Between activities I tried to always find time for a quick stop at the bookstore. Since I was racing against the clock to secure funding, it seemed imperative to work weekend evenings as well.

There was so much I didn't know, and I wanted to learn as much as possible before I went down to the Atlanta conference. Desperate for information, I ordered dozens of audiotapes from prior education conferences. I listened to the tapes each morning on the treadmill, hoping to get practical advice, but most of them turned out to be theoretical presentations about the politics of education reform, or focused on narrow subjects like a specific method for assessing literacy. I was learning a lot, but what I really needed was a how-to guide to execute on my idea of starting a system of schools.

The problem was that almost no information was available on starting a charter in New York, let alone a nonprofit system of charter schools. The field barely existed.

Finally, on a Thursday morning in June, I listened to a presentation that blew me away. The voice on the tape was astute, kindhearted, and full of optimism. He was an educator, but he talked like an entrepreneur about market share, metrics, and growth models. I wanted to listen with my full attention, so I jumped off the treadmill but neglected to turn it off. I landed on the ground, and that's where I stayed until the end of the tape. The speaker's name was Don Shalvey. And I had to meet him.

In 1992, California had become the second state in the nation to pass a charter law, and Don Shalvey had established California's first charter school that same year. He was now starting to expand into a system of charters he had launched called Aspire Public Schools.

I called the operator and tracked down Don's number. He picked up on my first try and we spoke for about twenty minutes. I explained that I wanted to start a system of charter schools in New York, and I was seeking advice. "Do you have a business plan?" he asked. "No, not yet," I replied. "How about a charter?" "No, I've just started." "Do you have any funders?" "No, but I'm working on it." "What is your school design?" he asked. I stopped and took a breath. "My design is that there is no design," I replied. I sounded like an episode of *Seinfeld*.

"I want to give teachers more freedom, with the understanding that everyone is accountable for results," I told Don. "The whole concept of a 'school design' seems wrong to me—it's not the way to get the best out of people in any organization. I believe it's demeaning to mandate how a teacher should teach. I think we should change the way school systems are run entirely." I told Don about how I had been influenced by Peter Drucker's *Management Challenges in the 21st Century.*

Don said he was swamped trying to grow his Aspire network of schools, but he was intrigued and wanted to help. I was elated. "Why don't you write up an executive summary of your plan, then we can talk next week," he suggested.

Of course, he'd meant over the phone. But I could sense from our call that he was very knowledgeable and I wanted to learn more from him. It just so happened that my kids were about to go to sleepaway camp for the month.

"I have so many questions," I said. "Do you think we could spend a few days together? I could come out to California next week." Don laughed. "I'll tell you what," he said. "Come on out the week after next. Meantime, start working on your executive summary."

I booked a flight, and I got to work.

The purpose of the executive summary would be to secure funding. I didn't want to scare away funders by coming across as flaky with my idea that focusing on teachers would save public education. They would expect me to describe product features like class size or school size, length of the day, type of curriculum. That's what a detailed school design looked like. I imagined that's what Don probably expected.

But my idea did not fit into this mold. I was not answering the question "What is your school design?" I was changing the question. The question I wanted to answer was "How do you make teachers excellent?" I began typing.

"What we need is a complete paradigm shift," I wrote. "We will never fix education in America by trying to figure out the single best product design, then imposing it on teachers and mandating their compliance. We need to stop dictating teaching methods and curriculum. Instead, we need to figure out how to cultivate the passion and talent of teachers." Maybe it sounded simplistic, but it was all I had figured out so far—and it was what I planned to share with Don.

The night before my flight, I prepared a list of fifty-five questions, and organized them into the same categories as my school startup task list.

I could barely contain my excitement when I arrived at Don's offices in Silicon Valley. The first thing I saw was a profile of him from the *Wall Street Journal* posted near the entrance. Don showed me around and introduced me to his team of nine staffers.

Then we spent all morning in his conference room, as he talked about how he planned to grow Aspire into a larger system of charter schools. Don sketched out his five-year plan on a large whiteboard. "There are only a small handful of us doing this work," he said. "The first thing to think about is your growth model. Do you want to grow fast through a franchise model, or do you want to directly manage your schools?" I started to think about that question, but he quickly moved on to others.

"Will you be a full K through twelve school district or operate just elementary schools? Most charters start with kindergarten—it's so much easier. Will you be the first principal or will you hire from the outside?" It occurred to me that I had to be the first principal. How could I presume to guide schools in the future if I didn't roll up my sleeves and serve as a principal myself?

Don went on to talk about measuring results, recruiting teachers, and not overlooking the importance of community relations. "And you need to take on fundraising, which is an enormous challenge. But the most daunting task you will face, Deborah, is facility development. It's all about real estate, Deborah. If you don't have facilities, you won't have schools."

Facilities? I didn't even have a charter! Still, I tried to listen carefully to absorb all of Don's valuable advice, furiously taking notes so I could review the information again later.

At the end of the day, I asked Don if he would join my advisory board. Luckily, he agreed to join without inquiring who else was on it, because I had just created it at that moment. "And I'm going to tell Kim Smith about you," Don said. About two years earlier, Kim had started the NewSchools Venture Fund, a foundation that provided early support for education startups.

Over the next four days, I went everywhere with Don. I observed him as he conducted a walk-through of one of his schools, popping into classrooms and giving informal feedback to the principal. I sat in on a meeting as he worked with his chief operating officer to finalize a fundraising presentation.

And I tagged along at night as he convinced the Stockton town council to allow him to build a school facility. Don needed them to change the zoning classification of one area from residential to educational so that he could build a school there. They were extremely wary of this proposal at the beginning of the hearing, but he gained their trust through his soft, deferential tone and his respectful answers to all of their questions. By the end of the evening, he had convinced the entire community board to vote in his favor.

We were on the road for hours every day. At one point, we visited Don's mother. On the way there, we stopped at a gas station and Don picked up potato chips and Diet Coke for lunch. On the way back, he stopped to give me a tour of the orchards he owned behind his new home. We picked fresh fruit—he was growing organic grapes, peaches, and figs. Don laughed as I gathered up as much fruit as I could, holding it all with the bottom of my shirt.

As we zipped from meeting to meeting, Don told me about his

background as a guidance counselor and school superintendent, and talked about how he started Aspire. I soon discovered that Aspire was the first organization of its kind in the country: a system of public schools that would later become known as a "CMO" or charter management organization. This was exactly what I wanted to start in Harlem. I was hoping to create a parallel system that would eventually become a model for how to redesign the American school system.

As Don drove me to the airport to catch the red-eye back to New York at the end of the week, I was exhilarated. "There are hundreds of things to do, Deborah" he said. "You already know that. But the single most important thing you need is stamina. Startups are tough, and growth is tougher. On top of that, the anti-charter politics turn this into an uphill battle every day. They put roadblocks in front of us every step of the way. And just when you've overcome one crisis, another one hits you. You need resilience for a startup—the will to just keep going."

It was getting late. Don stopped the car at the airport parking lot, and we got out to say good-bye. He opened the trunk and handed me a document from a cardboard box. It was a copy of his business plan. "You need to develop your own plan, Deborah. It's going to be really hard and you're going to make tons of mistakes. I make mistakes every day—we're leaking oil all over the place! But I know you can do this. You have the fire in you."

I still had no startup funding. I still had to write that huge charter application. And I still had to figure out how to create a school system from scratch. But at least I knew that someone else in the country was doing it. Meeting Don made my dream feel possible. And I no longer felt completely alone.

Back in New York, I poured my heart into writing the business plan. Since the kids were at summer camp, I took over the family room and dining room. My command center was stacked with books and papers, half-empty cups of tea, and a ridiculous amount of Coke. In just two weeks they would return home, and I'd want to focus all of my time on them, getting them ready for the new school year. So I worked around the clock.

"Our nation has a fundamentally flawed strategy when it comes to public education," I wrote in the introduction to my business plan late one night. "The most essential element in effective schools is effective people. Our strategy will be a dramatic shift from 'product replication' to 'people development.' The distinction is profound." To emphasize the point, I created a chart:

Developing People	Replicating Product
Empower People	Get "Buy-In" / Sell Product
Develop & Support People	Support Product Implementation
Accountability	Quality Control / Compliance

I explained my strategy in detail. "Our teachers will be empowered to select curriculum and instructional methods. This level of ownership will attract the best and brightest, unleash their passion and engender exceptional performance."

The weeks flew by. Late on a Sunday morning, I rushed to get the house ready for the kids, picking up papers, files, and books off the family room floor, off the coffee table, and off the dining room table. They would be coming home from camp in the afternoon and I couldn't wait to meet them at the bus, but I had to get the place organized and to clear my mind so I could focus on them.

For the next few days, the kids played outside and finished up their summer reading while I filled out dozens of school forms, made shopping lists, and marked up the large family calendar that I kept on the refrigerator with all of the kids' activities: choir, religious school, Girl Scouts, soccer, baseball, math team, science club, chess club. The beginning of the new school year was around the corner. We drove to Staples to buy pencil cases, notebooks, and everything else on their school supply lists. This year, Avi also needed some camping gear, as he would be spending the first few days of September at a program called Nature's Classroom.

All three kids were now in middle school: Rachel in fifth grade, Chava in sixth, and Avi in seventh. The girls came home from their first day excited to tell me that they loved their new teachers. Avi was off at Nature's Classroom with the entire seventh grade and I wouldn't hear from him all week. We were starting to settle back into our routine.

A few days later, on the morning of September 11, 2001, I was getting ready to go into the city for a meeting. But I never got on the train. A friend called me at nine to ask if I'd heard. "Are you watching the news?" she asked. "No, I'm getting ready to leave. Why?" "Oh my God, turn on the TV." I ran downstairs to take the TV out of the closet and quickly turned it on. I was in shock, and glued to the television, along with the rest of the nation.

My flight to the Atlanta conference on September 24, 2001, was early, and security, understandably, took hours. Soon I would be meeting hundreds of people from around the country who were committed to education reform. Hopefully, I'd also meet funders so that I could start schools for children who had no access to quality education. I tried to ignore my looming deadlines and focus on the task at hand.

I didn't know anything about the Education Leaders Council, and knew almost no one at the conference, so I was happy to run into my old boss, Chris Whittle from Edison, at lunch. "I'm surprised to see *you* here!" he said. I wasn't sure what he meant, but I quickly found out. A woman with lots of makeup wearing a St. John suit pulled up a chair to chat with us. She joked derisively about limousine liberals and made an offhand comment about how the Democrats were a "wholly owned subsidary of the teachers' union." The lunch speaker, a Republican congressman, made fun of progressives who criticized teaching to the test. "When I was in grade school, I had to take a spelling test every Friday. So my teacher taught me how to spell! What's wrong with that?" he said to laughter and applause from the audience.

It would be an understatement to say that I didn't identify as a conservative, but there was no question that this Republican gathering was passionately championing the next phase of the civil rights movement: educational equality for low-income children. While one could argue the merits and limitations of testing, which this group supported, it was undeniable that they cared about the children whose lives were being ruined by a failed education system. They were on the side of the children on this issue. My perception of social justice as a Democratic ideal was being challenged—first at Edison, and now here.

Unless I was misunderstanding something, it seemed that the union had influenced the Democratic establishment to actively fight *against* enabling disenfranchised parents to choose a quality school for their children, *against* the expansion of quality charter schools, and *against* equal rights for minorities. It was shameful.

For two days I attended sessions, and talked with school district superintendents, elected officials, and nonprofit leaders. But I hadn't met a single potential funder, and I was beginning to despair.

At a cocktail reception on the final night of the conference I met Chester Finn—a renowned conservative education scholar who looked serious and sounded intimidating. I soon learned that everyone called him Checker, and that he had been the assistant secretary of education under President Reagan.

Once we started speaking with one another, we lost all interest in the party. "What you're describing is not a new kind of school—it's a new kind of public school *system*," he said, as I explained my concept. "Exactly!" I replied. It was such a relief to hear someone really understand my idea. Checker invited me to sit with him at dinner, and by the end of the night, we had gotten to know each other pretty well. As we stood up to leave the dinner, Checker paused for a moment. He looked at me and said, "There's someone who should know about you. Do you have a card?"

The conference was over but I had arranged a late afternoon flight so I could visit the Dr. Martin Luther King Jr. museum and memorial in downtown Atlanta. As I waited in the lobby of the hotel for a shuttle, I ran into Kim Smith, of the NewSchools Venture Fund, and her colleague. They were headed to the King Center as well—what a perfect coincidence.

Don Shalvey had told me there were only a handful of charter funders and Kim was at the forefront. She knew everyone, and everyone wanted to know her. If I had any chance at all to be funded, this could be it.

At the King Center, I found myself staring at the photos of the famous Woolworth's lunch counter sit-in in Greensboro, North Carolina, which had taken place on February 1, 1960, two years to the day before Joel was born. Joel had met one of the young men years later at an academic retreat, and he told Joel that they had fully expected to be killed. As I looked at the photos, I wondered what it felt like to be willing to die for a cause. I wondered if those courageous young men had a sense of how dramatically they'd shape history. And I wondered if they would have been sad to know that forty years later, our nation had still not attained equality when it came to a fundamental civil right: a quality education.

I went outside and sat by the reflecting pool with Kim. Before I knew it, we were discussing my business plan, and she was shooting rapid-fire questions. "Do you have any other funders? Do you have a charter? Who's on your board? What will you do about facilities? Is New York City supportive?"

Then the questions turned more conceptual: "What is your core strategy? What makes you different? How do you plan to succeed where others have failed?" I answered, and she shot back with more questions. Then Kim stood up and said to her colleague, "Well, this is exactly what I've been talking about. Deborah wants to change the system."

I smiled calmly, but inside I was ecstatic. This could be the seed funding I needed! I asked her about timing.

Kim explained that they were still in the process of finalizing the next round of their own funding, and they'd be ready to start making new investments next spring. "Let's wait and see. We may be able to fly you out in February to make a formal presentation and pitch your idea."

I was instantly deflated. I didn't want to sound desperate—nobody wants to invest in someone who is desperate—but that's exactly what I was. In order to be considered for their new portfolio, she said, I'd need to have more in place: an initial team, a business plan, charters approved, a list of other potential funders, and more.

It was a lot of work, and I was willing to do it. But I couldn't wait until next spring. my whole plan would fall apart if I didn't raise funding in the next few months. I wasn't sure how—or if—to tell her.

I arrived early to the Atlanta airport. With a few hours to wait, I went to the bookstore where I noticed a display for a new book. *Jack: Straight from the Gut*, written by Jack Welch, the legendary CEO of General Electric, had just come out. Welch had appeared on many magazine covers in recent years and *Fortune* magazine had named him "the manager of the century."

I sat down with a cup of tea and the book and almost missed my flight because I was so immediately engrossed. I loved that he talked about his disdain for bureaucracy and "artificial congeniality." His notion of "making people your core competency" energized me, and I scribbled notes in the margins about how to apply his ideas to school systems.

Then, about a hundred pages in, I discovered something that made my heart skip a beat. Jack Welch actually knew Peter Drucker! In fact, Drucker, the person who had inspired my "people, not product" education strategy, had been a mentor to Welch shortly after he became CEO of GE, and Welch attributed many of his big ideas to his sessions with Drucker. A few years later, after his death in 2005, *BusinessWeek* would put Drucker on the cover with the headline "The Man Who Invented Management," and Welch would praise him as the greatest management thinker of the twentieth century.

I didn't know what I was more excited about: Welch's connection to Peter Drucker, or Welch's ideas. For example, he wrote about Work-Out, a practice that would later become integral to our schools. Work-Out was an open meeting where his employees spoke candidly about whatever was getting in the way of improving their businesses, and Jack wrote that it had transformed his company.

The rationale for Work-Out "could be summed up by the comment made by a middle-aged appliance worker: 'For twenty-five years,' he said, 'you've paid for my hands when you could have had my brain as well—for nothing.' Work-Out confirmed what we already knew," Welch wrote, "that the people closest to the work know it best."

That was just it! *Teachers know the work best.* So why was it so difficult for our nation's leaders to trust teachers? Welch was treating his factory workers with more respect than our schools were treating their teachers.

I decided that our schools would have a workout to replace the old, bureaucratic-style faculty meetings that most schools filled with boring administrative announcements. At our workout, our teachers would be able to bring up problems, collaborate with the principal, brainstorm solutions on the spot, and feel comfortable to share candid feedback. We would cut through bureaucracy and get stuff done.

Soon it was October, and I was starting to worry, as it didn't look like any seed funding would come through in time. I was working late one night in the basement when the phone rang. "Hi, this is Tom Vander Ark. Checker Finn told me about you," he said. "Hi," I said to Tom. (Oh my God! I said to myself.)

Tom was executive director of education at the Bill and Melinda Gates Foundation. Gates had recently hired him to start making education grants, but there was no formal application process. Actually, there was no way to apply at all. They did their own research, and they had to hear about you.

"Checker said that I had to meet you. I'll be in New York next week, if you'd like to have dinner?"

We met for dinner at six o'clock at Tao on East Fifty-Eighth Street. We were seated with a view of a giant sixteen-foot Buddha statue and the restaurant was packed. I learned that he believed the key to education reform was small school size, close relationships between adults and students, and a curriculum that was relevant to real life. Tom told me that his average grant was about $1 million and that he had a lean staff consisting of an associate and an assistant.

He had no bureaucracy and an enormous amount of money to give away. I liked this guy!

I had prepared an executive summary, but I never took it out of my bag. We started talking and before I knew it, two hours had gone by. But in the course of the evening, Tom told me three things that made it clear that my chances of startup funding were slim to none.

First, he had never funded someone with no school. All his other grantees were renowned educators, running the most highly acclaimed high schools in the country. There was Dennis Littky, the founder of the Met High School in Providence, Rhode Island, who had a dual Ph.D. in psychology and education, and who had been profiled in a book that became an NBC movie. Larry Rosenstock, founder of High Tech High in San Diego, had been an attorney, a teacher, and a school principal. And, of course, there was Don Shalvey. All of them had decades of experience in school leadership. Tom had been traveling the country like a talent scout, visiting and evaluating schools, and giving out grants to the leaders with the most potential.

Second, Tom hadn't funded anyone in New York City without an intermediary. I didn't even know what that meant. He explained that because the Gates Foundation had such a massive amount of money, they partnered with other foundations, like NewSchools Venture Fund, to help them distribute it. The smaller foundations served as intermediaries by evaluating prospective grantees, making decisions about whom to fund, and monitoring the results. I mentioned that I had met NewSchools founder Kim Smith in Atlanta, and Tom told me that she was pitching him to give her a grant so she could become one of his intermediaries.

Finally, he was funding high schools exclusively, but I had planned to start from kindergarten. "Almost all the charters in the country are elementary schools," he argued. "We need people who are willing to take on the challenge of high school." Tom insisted that I should open high schools, that they were the most difficult, important, and neglected element of education reform. We both knew that it was easier to start with younger children.

I described my "people not product" strategy and my passionate belief in teachers. By the time our tea arrived, it was almost 9:30 p.m. As I took my first sip, Tom looked straight at me. "I want to give you a grant to start schools," he said.

What?! A grant from the Gates Foundation? That's at least a million dollars.

"There are a few things you'll need to do for the grant to become final," he said. "You'll need to be approved for at least two charters. Also, since you don't have a school, you'll need to send me a business plan that Bill Gates Sr. will review, and he'll have to approve it."

Two charters at once? New York state had never granted two simultaneous charters, and I would be new and unproven. Another problem was that New York would not approve a charter unless you could demonstrate that you had a reliable funding commitment.

It was a catch-22: I needed the charters to get the funding, but I needed funding to get the charters.

"I'm gathering all our grantees next month," Tom said. "You're not an official grantee yet, so you'll attend as a guest. The smartest educators in the country will be there."

"Sounds amazing," I said. "I'd love to join you. Where's the conference?"

"Providence," he answered.

CHAPTER 5

A SCHOOL FOR
MY CHILDREN

SIDWELL FRIENDS IS KNOWN AS ONE of the finest schools in the nation. The Clintons chose this private school in Washington, D.C., for Chelsea, and the Obamas later sent their two girls as well. My vision for my students in Harlem was quite simple: they deserved the same world-class education.

In a few weeks I'd be traveling to the conference in Providence, and I had a feeling Tom would start asking more specific questions about my vision. I decided to spend a few weeks visiting the best private schools in the Northeast. The first was the Sidwell Friends School.

In every classroom I observed at Sidwell, students were engaged in sophisticated analytical discussions, debating their ideas with confidence. I wanted our classrooms in Harlem to feel like this. I wanted to walk through our schools and see our students puzzling over a difficult passage of reading, or strategizing an approach to a complex mathematical problem. As we would write in our charter applications, I wanted our teachers to refrain from providing conclusions as starting points, but rather insist that students assemble valid evidence to reach their own conclusions.

But what I really loved about Sidwell was its core belief that the purpose of a school is to help students live in accordance with timeless values like simplicity, service, and compassion. This emphasis on values was precisely what I wanted for my own children's education. I wanted Avi, Chava, and Rachel to be avid readers, intellectually sophisticated, wholesome in character, and fiercely independent thinkers. And above all, I wanted them to be compassionate, to care about people. I imagined that the parents I would come to know in Harlem would want the same for their children.

Sidwell Friends was a model of education at the very highest level. Bringing this private-school standard to my school—and eventually to all urban schools—was my dream. But turning it into a reality would be extremely challenging.

For one, our schools would be constrained by the state testing regimen. I believed that the most important things that we need to teach children can't be measured by standardized tests. Good test scores, however, would be required in order to keep our charters. And that would be all the more challenging because we'd be enrolling students whose former schools did not teach them the basics. How could they focus on analyzing a great book when so many of our incoming students wouldn't know how to read at grade level or capitalize the beginning of a sentence? Behavior would also be a major issue. So many of the public school teachers I'd observed were forced to devote all of their energy to disciplining students who hadn't been trained in basic classroom decorum.

After a day observing classes, I went to the main office to meet with the headmaster. As I waited, reading Sidwell's brochure for parents of prospective students, a mother of a sixth grader asked me if I was planning to enroll my child in the school.

"Actually, I do have three kids, but we live in New York," I said. "I'm starting schools in Harlem and I'm visiting here to get ideas." She had one of those looks on her face like she was trying to be polite but I could tell she was dubious. "Well that's very nice," she said. "And where do your kids go to school?"

Suddenly my excitement about Sidwell as an inspiration for my Harlem school turned to guilt over what this new direction in my life would mean for my own children. I could send my kids to an exceptional private school like this if I pushed off my Harlem school project for eight years and took a corporate job. But starting a nonprofit meant I would have to keep them in public school and cut back significantly on family travel and other expenses. The public schools in Westchester were good, but I could provide them with an even better education if I sent them to a private school.

Was this fair to my own children? Didn't my children deserve the best school that I could provide for them? Or did I owe it to all children—especially the disenfranchised—to try to make urban public schools as excellent as private schools?

As I left the campus late that afternoon, walking along the front lawn down to the street, I started reading the Quaker "Testimonies" that the headmaster had given me. One question spoke to me: Do you live in peace with yourself?

That night, still anxious, I prayed and thought about that question. What would Joel say, I wondered.

Just before falling asleep, I felt the answer. "Relax, they will be fine," he would have told me. "The best education you can give them will be the example you set."

Yes, I was sure he would say they'd be fine. Start a school. Challenge the system. Keep going.

The first person I met at the Gates conference was wearing a tie-dyed T-shirt with a neon peace sign, a rainbow-colored kaffiyeh, and black jeans—and he was one of the most celebrated education reformers at this gathering of superstars. Dennis Littky, also known simply as Doc, was famous for his radical approach to education. When I walked in, Dennis was deep in conversation with Larry Rosenstock, the innovative founder of High Tech High in San Diego.

Tom walked over and put his arms around Dennis and Larry. "I see you've met the smartest educators in the country," he gushed. "You'll hear about the school Dennis created later today. His graduation rates are through the roof, his dropouts went from twenty percent to two percent." Of course, I was immediately interested. "Why do you have so few dropouts?" I asked Dennis. "Kids drop out because school is fucking boring," he said. "And they drop out because they feel like nobody cares about them. When you connect a kid with a subject he's passionate about and an adult who cares, you're doing much more than just educating them. We're helping kids to transform themselves."

It didn't take more than fifteen minutes in the room for me to realize that most of the educators in this group were the philosophical and political opposite of those at the Education Leaders Council. The Gates Foundation had gathered an incredibly smart and sophisticated group that reminded me of the counselors and educators at my summer camp. These were the progressive educators who represented the prevailing view in American schools—the view that I had encountered at Teachers College, rooted in John Dewey's philosophy of experiential learning. They were, in fact, the very liberals that the conservatives I met at the Atlanta conference made fun of. These guys pushed right back, deriding the conservatives for dumbing down the curriculum and teaching to the test.

Both groups embraced the autonomy afforded by the charter movement. But that's just about where the similarities ended. The conservative approach to education reform was focused on standards, testing, teacher evaluation, and a "back to basics" curriculum. The Gates group believed in small school size and close student-teacher relationships. They argued that students learned best through projects, and that assessment should be through exhibitions and research papers, not fill-in-the-bubble tests.

Dennis had spent years practicing these ideals. After he finished his doctoral courses at the University of Michigan, he got an offer to work as a school psychologist and community organizer at a high school in the Ocean Hill–Brownsville section of Brooklyn in 1969. His parents had read about the violent confrontations that had landed Ocean Hill–Brownsville on the cover of *Newsweek*, and they didn't want him to go. Dennis took the job anyway, and was one of the only white teachers among a mostly black staff and student body.

At twenty-seven, he was tapped to be a school principal in Shoreham, Long Island. "They let me run the school my way," he told me. What was his way? "We had a farm in back so kids could learn by doing. I created an advisory system and I broke up the large school of six hundred kids into smaller houses of two hundred each. All of that was so every kid had a personal connection to a caring adult," he explained. "Kids need more than skills. We created internships and personalized learning plans. You need to teach kids how to persevere, to be able to overcome obstacles."

"To me, it was all just common sense, man," Dennis said. "When kids get their shit together, they can do amazing things. They just need us to allow them to discover what they love and learn about that."

Dennis was fearless about doing things his way—and that included taking on the education establishment. Once, while he was busy turning around a failing New Hampshire high school, he heard that Ted Sizer, chair of Brown University's education department, was giving a lecture about how to improve schools. Curious to hear what Sizer would say, Dennis, who by that point had turned around several failing schools, showed up for the talk. After the lecture, Dennis told me,

"I went up to him and said, 'All your radical ideas—you're just talking about it, I'm doing it. Get your ass down to my school.' Then I ran outside and threw up."

Dennis's story with Ted Sizer didn't end at that first encounter. Ted took Dennis up on his invitation, and once he saw what Dennis was doing in New Hampshire, he selected his school as the first in his new organization, the Coalition of Essential Schools, a group that promoted progressive educational principles. "Debbie's school was next," Dennis said, referring to the educator Debbie Meier, who was renowned for running the Central Park East School in East Harlem.

Ten years later, the education commissioner of Rhode Island approached Dennis and asked him to open a school. And now the Gates Foundation had asked him to do ten more. He worked seven days a week, twelve hours a day. "You can see how fucking hard it is, man." Yes, I could.

I loved his drive and passion, and his sense of humor. During the last session that night, we were sitting together when I started a task list. I wrote "To Do" on top of the notepad, then I got up to get a cookie. When I returned, I saw that Dennis had added his name to the list.

As I walked into breakfast the next morning I was happy to see Don Shalvey. "Hi, Deborah, join us," Don said enthusiastically. He was sitting with Larry Rosenstock. I asked Larry how he started High Tech High. "It all began in the summer of '96," he said. Larry had received a federal grant to study the practices of high-poverty urban high schools that were getting kids into college. "I immediately called Ted and Debbie to ask if they'd be part of it—and they said yes. We had a war room in Cambridge for three years. It was insane!" (Although they weren't at the conference with us, the influence of Ted Sizer and Debbie Meier was felt in that room.)

Then I asked Larry about his schools and his philosophy. "Diversity and innovation matter," he said, "And small school size matters. You don't see any private high schools with two thousand kids because the social unit maxes out at three hundred fifty, four hundred." School size was a constant theme at this conference.

"And schools need socioeconomic integration," he continued. "It bothers me that the cultural pluralism narrative of New York City has vanished. I agree with Jefferson, who created the first nonsectarian university on the planet in 1819, the University of Virginia. He said the purpose of public education isn't to serve the public, it's to make a public. Like Dewey believed, the purpose of public education isn't to replicate society, it's to transform society."

What the . . . ?! School size to integration to Jefferson to John Dewey, practically without taking a breath. I'd soon learn that this was classic Larry—telling stories with tangents upon tangents, integrating politics, history, sociology, and education.

Tom was right. He had selected a group of superstars, Dennis and Don and Larry foremost among them.

But some school leaders at the Gates conference seemed to talk about nothing but their anti-testing attitude. One principal told me that she'd organized her students to protest the New York State Regents exams. "The tests are a mile wide and an inch deep," she told me. "They make it impossible to teach in a meaningful way. They force students to memorize information." I asked her how she would propose to hold schools accountable, and her reply was emphatic: college acceptance rates.

But I wondered if college acceptance alone was a valid measure of high school quality, since so many students who were accepted into college needed remedial coursework.

I agreed that the tests were far from perfect, and I considered it a worthy mission to improve test quality. But I questioned if students were best served by spending their time protesting against the test rather than learning the skills on the test. I also believed that some memorization could be a valuable intellectual exercise.

I was determined not to let the tests define the curriculum in my schools. But I did not accept that testing would completely inhibit a teacher's ability to teach at a high level.

In Providence, it was impossible not to be turned on by the vision of people like Larry and Dennis. But my own children were now in middle school, and I was witnessing firsthand the potential pitfalls of progressive education. One afternoon, Avi came home asking me for magazines. "There are some old magazines in the recycling bin in the garage," I said. "What are they for?"

He told me that he had to make a poster. "It's project learning," he said. "Okay, hon. What are you learning?" I asked. "Nothing," he replied. "It's just a poster." I wanted to believe he was learning something, but when I looked closely at his assignment, I saw that he was right. The teacher may have labeled this assignment as "project-based learning," but it was really just fluff.

Of course, this was a poor execution of an educational project. Tom had told me about the cutting-edge projects at High Tech High, where Larry's students built robots and presented their findings during open forums called exhibitions. But without a smart teacher, this approach could easily devolve into nonsense.

In other words, I believed progressive education was superior—as long as it was executed well. And that was dependent on quality people.

Back in New York, my priority was still to apply for the charters. My six-month deadline was nearing—I started to count down in weeks instead of months.

At the suggestion of someone I'd met at the Gates conference, I hired Sarah, a former Boston charter school principal, as a consultant. She promptly recruited Andrew, who had been a Columbia University graduate student, as a weekend volunteer. Andrew was cerebral, fun, and witty. And he shared my work ethic. He eventually became the key architect of the academic portion of our charter applications.

Andrew and I spent a lot of time together in what he called Socratic dialogues. I shared my ideas and he crafted the most beautiful prose. We'd have long talks at coffee shops in the city and on the deck of my home in Dobbs Ferry. Andrew got to know my children and he shared my educational vision. We talked endlessly about how to actually provide private school quality education for students in underserved communities. We were not just creating a document to secure the charter or to sell ourselves to funders. We were serious about our aspirations for changing public education.

Ultimately, in the charter applications and business plan, our vision was described as somewhat of a dream:

> Imagine a school where students work so intensely that the world outside the essay or problem or experiment before them seems muffled and far away. Their work leaves them sweaty, exhausted and satisfied. They take their work home not because somebody told them that it's homework, but because it's theirs, they can't leave it behind, they're not done with it yet. The problem still needs solving, or the question must be figured out.

> Our academies will be a place where students work hard and love it, just as a real athlete is entirely immersed in her game, or a serious musician gets perfectly lost in his music. A place where students look forward to reading a challenging book, completing a difficult math equation, pushing their limits each day.

As they pursue a demanding course of study, we want our students to think critically, argue passionately, and take ownership of their learning.

We want our students to ask and understand hard questions about texts. We want them to develop habits of logical and analytical thinking, to understand the underlying premise of a mathematical procedure, to train and push their minds. It isn't enough to be able to write a five-paragraph essay. They must have full command of every element of the writing process, understanding the logic behind grammatical conventions, and the appropriate usage of advanced vocabulary.

We believe a complete education includes the nurturing of a wholesome character and universal moral virtues. We hope that each student will cultivate friendships marked by dignity and compassion. We understand that values can not be dictated or imposed through programs but must ensue from immersion in a school environment where those values are authentically lived and modeled on a daily basis.

We are persuaded that the marks of a successful student are precise thought, the ability to speak rationally and write clearly, summoning evidence to support one's arguments, the willingness to examine the grounds of one's arguments, and to accede graciously, when appropriate, to stronger opinions. The mastery of these habits of scholarship simultaneously requires and fosters the intellectual capacity and moral virtues necessary for students to become active and thoughtful democratic citizens.

I wanted our schools to offer the rich intellectual experiences that Larry and Dennis and Debbie and Ted believed in. Their vision was inspiring. It was what I had seen at the private schools I'd visited. It was what I wanted for my own children and what I wanted for our Harlem children. At the same time, my first responsibility would be to make sure that the students who came into our schools far behind grade level would catch up on the basics in reading, writing, and math. I was sure we could do both. We had to.

CHAPTER 6

DOWN TO THE WIRE

I WAS WORKING FURIOUSLY around the clock toward three deadlines: the business plan that Bill Gates Sr. would review in January, the charter applications due in early March, and the NewSchools Venture Fund presentation coming up just after Dr. Martin Luther King Day. These tasks each had to be executed flawlessly, and I needed a funding commitment from Gates or NewSchools for the charters to be approved.

I continued to call Don, Larry, and other school leaders I'd met. They couldn't have been more generous with advice about everything from teacher recruiting to school facilities. The latter became Larry's mantra: Every time I called he'd answer the same way: "DKNY! Do you have a building yet?"

But I also needed someone who could help me navigate the complicated bureaucracy of education politics in New York City, where the first few charter schools had been operating for only two years. According to all of my friends, Sy Fliegel of the Center for Educational Innovation was the guy who knew everything and everyone in New York City education. Sy had been a maverick school district superintendent, and he knew how to work through—and sometimes around—bureaucracy.

One bitterly cold morning I took the train into the city to meet Sy at his offices on West Forty-Fourth Street. When I arrived, Sy introduced me to his colleague Harvey Newman, who had been a school principal. The three of us sat down, and Harvey and Sy told me about the small schools that they and other reformers, including Debbie Meier, had started in East Harlem in the 1970s: alternative public schools that were colocated inside larger public school buildings.

Sy was like a caring, clever uncle. He had clearly done and seen it all. He and his colleagues had championed school choice for parents long before the charter movement came on the scene. His East Harlem district gave parents the power to choose their child's school—a free-market concept that was radical in its time.

Since his schools didn't have the autonomy from the teachers' union that charters provided, Sy told his school leaders to practice what he called "creative noncompliance" with the union. What was creative noncompliance exactly? Sy explained it by telling the story of a teacher who had shown up in his district office one day with a transfer notice. According to union work rules, teachers had the right to teach in any school they pleased and this teacher was there to inform Sy that he would now be teaching in his district! Sy asked the teacher why he wanted to teach in East Harlem. "I requested the transfer because it was the only way I was going to avoid getting an unsatisfactory rating," the teacher told him. Sy knew that he was required to take transfers based on union rules but he had no intention of complying. He looked at the teacher and said flat out, "Well you can't teach here. Take this notice back to your old district and tell them we have no position open here." He was a rule breaker. And I loved him for it.

"Sy covered us," said Harvey, who had been a school leader under

Sy. In the mid 1970s, Harvey was leading the East Harlem Block School on 108th Street. "I had a teacher who was terrible. He was the nicest person in the world, but the worst teacher in the world. I kept trying to support him to become a better teacher but he was just not capable. I told him to take two weeks off and to find a job, any job. I just couldn't let him teach in my school," Harvey told me. "But he was so well-liked amongst the staff that they came to me about him. I told them that I understood why they were upset, but I asked each of those teachers, imagine that your child was to have this teacher. How would you feel? That ended the meeting. They understood."

The key, Harvey said, was that Sy backed him up. "He protected all of us so that we could run good schools despite the union regulations. What's really frustrating is that nothing has changed," said Harvey. "The rules are the same today: If you want to get rid of a bad teacher, it takes you years and years, it consumes you. There are hearings and appeals and more hearings and constant evaluations, and the union always nails you on a procedural detail. The union makes it impossible to fire teachers for incompetence."

"Thank goodness you'll be a charter so you won't have these constraints," Sy said. Then he asked me, "What is your governance structure?" I wasn't sure exactly what he meant, but it sounded important. "You need to have control over your schools, Deborah. If you set up your board incorrectly, you could end up with a disaster." Sy told me about a well-intentioned school leader who had mistakenly set up his board as a partnership with a local community group that had a competing agenda. They constantly fought with him because they were more interested in their group's priorities than the school's needs, and as a result of this ongoing conflict with the board, the school was struggling.

I appreciated the warning, but Sy's story also made me nervous: I wondered about all the other things I didn't yet know that could cause me to fail. "Is there any course or handbook on how to start a charter school?" I asked. "Something that outlines all the pitfalls to avoid, the keys to success, and maybe a comprehensive task list?"

He looked at me like I'd just uttered the most naïve question he'd ever heard. "No, dear," Sy said patiently. "But I have something else for you. Then he got up, took a book off the shelf, autographed it, and handed it to me. On the train ride home, I started reading *Miracle in East Harlem*.

Sy also connected me to the Charter School Resource Center, a new group with three employees that had recently formed to help aspiring school leaders with charter applications.

"Are you applying to SUNY or SED?" Gerry asked at our first meeting, referring to the two charter authorizers in the state, the State University of New York and the New York State Education Department.

"I'm not sure. I was thinking SUNY but only because I met the director in Atlanta. I didn't realize there was a difference between the two," I said.

"Wow, you have a lot to learn about how politics will affect your schools," he laughed. "You've definitely got to meet Tom Carroll."

Tom was a conservative education reformer who had played a key role in passing the charter law in Albany. He had held administrative positions in New York state government and was also in the process of starting his own charter school. When I met Tom, he stressed the importance of applying to the right authorizer. Many states establish a charter law where the only authorizer is the state education department. "That's like allowing McDonalds to authorize a Burger King on the same block!" Tom explained. "So the governor made sure New York would have two authorizers. When we were pushing to get the charter law passed, the union fought hard but lost this particular battle. But they won bigger ones, like limiting the number of charters and reducing the amount of public funding they receive."

Why, I asked, are they so determined to make it difficult to run good schools for kids who desperately need them?

"It's all about money and political power," Tom said bluntly. "The charter movement is coming along to prove that with entrepreneurial energy, accountability, and parental choice we can really improve public education. That's a huge competitive threat to the union monopoly."

The politics were distressing, to say the least. The fact that these elected officials and unions were literally wasting children's lives blew my mind. But I couldn't let myself get bogged down by frustration. "So it's better to go through SUNY?" I confirmed. "Definitely. The SUNY board is appointed by the governor, who is pro-charter, so they are very much in favor of charter schools. It's basically the opposite with the State Education Department. They report to the Regents, who are appointed by the state legislature, which is controlled by the teachers' union. They are elected or thrown out of office depending on whether they vote according to the union's demands."

Then Tom said something that sealed the deal. "Plus, the State Education Department doesn't really manage by performance. They're all about compliance. They're a bureaucracy, Deborah, plain and simple," That was all I needed to hear. I would only apply to SUNY.

I still had to learn more about what SUNY was looking for in an application, so I called on Bob Bellafiore, the director of SUNY's Charter Schools Institute whom I'd met briefly in Atlanta, and we arranged a time to get together. Bob had been Governor Pataki's first press secretary and chief spokesperson. "The governor was a trailblazer," Bob said to me over coffee at the Algonquin Hotel. He told me that the governor had pushed charter school law through the state senate in the middle of a cold December night two years before, despite ferocious union opposition. The measure had narrowly passed, and only because the governor had tied the new charter law to a pay raise for the state legislature.

Even though it wasn't an official interview, it definitely felt like one. Bob was asking a lot of questions about my background and plans. He made it clear that the written application was only part of the process. There was also a review panel comprised of education experts who would evaluate the applicants, decide whether they were qualified to open a school, and advise the SUNY board. Then there was the final interview with the SUNY board itself.

Qualifying was no easy feat. Bob told me that compared to other states, New York's authorization process was particularly rigorous. Volume one of the application had eleven sections with fifty-seven attachments, and volume two consisted of eight exhibits. The application covered every conceivable question about the proposed schools. There were entire sections filled with questions about the student schedule, staffing, hiring, professional development, testing, parent involvement, discipline, school calendar, extracurricular, special education, and remediation. It was endless.

The charter authorizer also required the applicant to put together detailed plans for the operational side. How would we handle technology? What about safety and security, governance, data, financial systems, breakfast and lunch, nursing, human resources, payroll, compliance, reporting, uniforms, fundraising, facility maintenance, purchasing, and insurance? All this would have to be in place to even be considered for approval.

On top of all that, I'd need to gather signatures to demonstrate local community support for the proposed school; establish a quality board of trustees; and develop a vast array of policies, such as a code of conduct, a student handbook, and an employee manual.

I could barely imagine getting all this done on time. But there was more: we needed to find a school building. As Don and Larry had warned me, charters did not receive buildings for their schools. Therefore the charter application asked us to describe a detailed, multi-year facility development plan. So I'd need to find, rent, and renovate a temporary facility to start the school during our startup years while enrollment was low. Then I'd need to find, purchase, rent, or build a permanent physical facility once the school reached full enrollment.

I would later learn that denying buildings to charters was a bargaining chip that many states had given to the unions in order to get charter laws passed. The unions had pushed hard for this provision; I was told that it was a key aspect of their strategy to weaken the charter school movement. By forcing charter leaders to divert precious time away from education to raise funds and develop a facility, they made it even more difficult for the nonunionized charter schools to take off and sustain themselves.

I threw myself into making sure every aspect of the charter application was outstanding. Kim at NewSchools Venture Fund had introduced me to Daniel, a young Goldman Sachs analyst with a Stanford MBA who had also worked at Edison Schools. Daniel taught me how to create financial models from scratch using Excel. I spent weeks with Daniel at his parents' apartment on the Upper West Side, mapping out a budget and a financial growth plan for our schools. Meanwhile, my neighbor David volunteered his real estate expertise and offered to help with the facility search.

The actual budget for the startup year and five subsequent years needed to be attached to our application, along with letters of commitment regarding external funds we would raise to make up for the gap between state funding and per-pupil costs. The authorizer asked about fundraising because they knew that charter leaders could not survive on state funding alone. There were four reasons for this. First, there were startup costs like paying for salaries and supplies before the school opened. Then there was the facility cost. Third, charter schools usually opened with one grade and grew enrollment one grade at a time, so they did not benefit from economies of scale in the early years. Finally, we were told that the per-pupil funding that charters got was lower than traditional public schools, so charter schools had to fundraise to make up the difference.

In order to produce an accurate financial projection, we had to talk with nearly a dozen experts in business and education to piece together our budget line by line, one snippet of information at a time.

While Daniel and I dealt with the budget process, Andrew and I had to answer hundreds of academic questions. I stated our "people, not product" strategy up front. Then I went on to describe a curriculum and program that I knew would change once we hired teachers.

Some of the questions I found myself addressing at 2 or 3 a.m. were difficult, some were ridiculous, but all had to be answered. When is your opening day? What is your enrollment plan? What is the rationale for your enrollment plan? What will your diploma requirements be? What will be your dress code policy? How will you comply with the charter law? (Um, by complying with it!)

We were also asked to describe why the school was needed. The requirement to prove that there was a need for such a school was beyond absurd. In 2000, 78 percent of eighth graders in the Harlem neighborhood where we proposed opening a middle school were failing reading and 87 percent were failing math. In fact, Harlem had been one of the worst-performing school districts in the nation for decades. When Robert Kennedy visited with community leaders in 1966, he said, "Clearly the most important problem in Harlem is education." But we still had to answer the question. So we wrote:

> These students are trapped in a system of haves and have-nots. Given the poor academic preparation received at a young age, it is no surprise that the high school dropout rate is extremely high. Without a quality education, these children will be destined to repeat the cycle of poverty. The situation is, by all measures, a state of emergency. Our children deserve better.

Far into the early morning hours, we'd email each other revisions to the charter applications and business plan, drafts of answers, questions for each other, and areas to be researched the next day. As we got particularly punchy one night at 1:30 a.m., with emails flying and the deadline looming, I signed my email, "Party on!" and that became the way we signed emails for months.

At one point when we were close to our deadline, Daniel went to Russia for a week, but I emailed him anyway. "You're nuts, Deborah!" he wrote. "I found an Internet café so here I am working on the charter applications in Moscow!"

As I spent my nights editing, my kids were growing, especially Rachel, who had shot up several inches. One afternoon we headed to the Gap to get her a new pair of jeans. We were talking at the cash register about her English class when the clerk told me that my credit card was denied. That had never happened to me before.

I had become so absorbed by the work that I hadn't realized I was running out of money. I asked the salesperson to put the jeans on hold, and told Rachel that I would go back to get them for her in a few days. Then I went home to figure out what to do.

I stayed up half the night putting together a timeline and figuring out my personal budget. I tried to calculate how much money I would need until the Gates grant and charter would (hopefully) come through. We were so close. Looking at the numbers, I realized that taking a part-time job might be the only way to get by. But that would mean we wouldn't finish the business plan and charter applications in time. As it was, between taking care of the kids and trying to start these schools from scratch, I was working eighteen hour days, sometimes more.

There was no possibility of a bank loan, because I had a mortgage to pay and no steady income. So the next day I called my neighbor

David, our volunteer real estate developer and soon-to-be school trustee (if we could only get the charter), to discuss the situation.

David offered to give me a personal loan. I was nervous, knowing that I would now be going into debt with each passing month. But I was far too deep into the process to stop now. It would be impossible to function each day if I thought about the risk I was taking, so I put the thought out of my mind. I accepted the loan, thanked David for his generosity, and kept going.

Meanwhile, my son Avi's thirteenth birthday—his Bar Mitzvah—was rapidly approaching. Planning the ceremony and party was not as complicated as the charter application, but it was certainly a significant undertaking and I wanted it to be a wonderful experience for him. We prepared a nice lunch, then a kids party at night, both in the all-purpose room of the synagogue.

I wanted my kids to understand that, even though some of their friends had fancier parties, larger homes, or more expensive cars, they were still living an incredibly privileged life. I looked for opportunities to teach them that we were already better off than 99 percent of people on the planet. If an ad came on the car radio for the lottery I would start a dialogue about money. "If we won the lottery, I wouldn't want to buy a bigger house when other people are starving. So what charity would you guys give the million dollars to?"

The Bar Mitzvah was harder than any of us expected, as it was impossible not to feel Joel's absence. At various points during the service, someone or other broke down crying. The uncles and grandfathers recited prayers but all of us felt the same thing: it should have been Joel standing up there next to his son.

Avi couldn't have made us prouder. In his speech, he said, "I understand that life is not about what we can get, it's more about what we can give. My mom always says to us, 'To whom much is given, much is required.' As I become an adult, I hope to fulfill my obligations to God, to my family, to my community, and to the world."

I felt grateful to everyone, particularly to the men in the family—cousins, uncles, my brother-in-law Chuck, my father and father-in-law, Joel's brothers—as they lifted my son on his chair high above the dancing crowd, singing and celebrating. We were there to celebrate Avi, my wonderful, sensitive, kind son.

And yet no matter how many other men were in the room, the one who mattered to him most was not.

Late that night, Avi and I were hanging out in the family room and I could tell he felt sad. "Av, are you okay?" I asked, and he broke down crying. "I miss Daddy." I usually tried to not cry in front of my kids, because I didn't want them to be burdened with my own sadness. But at this moment, on this day, I knew it was okay for him to realize that each one of us felt the same way. So I held him there for I don't know how long and let myself cry with him.

In about a month Bill Gates Sr. would review our business plan. I called Tom Vander Ark at Gates to let him know that the plan would be coming to him on time, and to remind him that securing two charters would require a letter of commitment from him about funding.

"All sounds good, Deborah. Just a heads-up that the folks at New-Schools are pitching me on the idea that we fund them instead of funding you directly," Tom said casually. "They would be the intermediary and would consider your request along with others. I haven't decided which way we're going to go yet. It's all up in the air . . ."

My heart stopped. This was not what we had discussed. Not even close. The NewSchools grant, if I even got it, would be a fraction of the Gates grant. It wouldn't be enough. Even if it held me over for a few months, I would have to spend the next year fundraising to make up the difference, instead of recruiting teachers and learning from experienced school leaders. And what if NewSchools decided not to fund me at all?

I was devastated. Somehow, I forced myself to think quickly. "I'll be on the west coast next month to make a presentation to NewSchools," I said. "How about we meet in Seattle and talk through my business plan in person?" I figured if I could get together with Tom in person, there would be a chance to convince him to stick with his original plan. "Sure, happy to see you," he said. There was still hope.

Just before Dr. Martin Luther King weekend, I got on a flight to California, where I was scheduled to make the pitch to Kim at New-Schools. Then I'd make a short stop in Seattle to make my case to Tom.

The NewSchools Venture Fund offices in San Francisco were sunny and bright, with big windows, lots of open space, and a huge conference room. I had rehearsed with Sarah, my consultant, the night before. This was the big day. I picked up a Zen tea at Starbucks and arrived early, in my usual winter attire, which Kim immediately pointed out was a "very New York" outfit. It was all black.

This was just about the only time I ever used PowerPoint for a presentation. Don and Larry had both told me that NewSchools expected lots of charts, graphs, and data. It was the opposite of my off-the-cuff style.

After the presentation, I had no idea if Kim would decide to provide seed funding. I left feeling completely unsure about whether the schools would ever get off the ground.

I got a call from my father as I headed to the airport to see Tom in Seattle. "I'm proud of you, baby!" he said. "It's great that you're going to have a face-to-face meeting."

Tom and I had breakfast at a Marriott. He asked me lots of questions about the business plan but gave me no indication of whether he was any closer to a decision. I was getting anxious.

Back in New York, I tried to put the funding problem out of my mind as we worked feverishly for weeks and weeks to finish the charter applications. We made several runs to Kinko's, filling box after box with the hundreds of pages the state required. At one point, I fell asleep right near the copy machine at Kinko's, sitting on top of a stack of boxes.

My kids helped me collate the applications, along with Eric, our next-door neighbor and my son's best friend, who used to hang out at our house all the time. For two nights in a row—my kids in PJs and me in gray sweatpants—we put the materials together. I wondered why the authorizer didn't allow electronic submission. It would have been so much more efficient to email a PDF. But that wasn't an option. We were submitting applications for two schools, and each application consisted of two binders filled with hundreds of pages of materials. They had to be organized in a precise manner in accordance with the authorizer's regulations, and they required ten hard copies of each, so that was forty binders in total to be copied and collated.

On March 8, 2002, we shipped off thousands of pages to Albany, with our prayers. Our final sentence was a plea to the authorizer. "We submit this application with a sense of urgency and a commitment to serve children who desperately need—and deserve—a quality education."

The charter application was a critical part of the process, but it was just the first step. We still had the formal interview with the charter authorizer—and it was coming up in about a month. We would need that funding commitment from either Gates or NewSchools in time for the interview or we would have no chance of being approved.

On a sunny Thursday afternoon at 4:30 the kids had just gone outside to ride their bikes, and I was in my basement office preparing for the interview when the phone rang. It was the NewSchools Venture Fund calling, and they got right to the point: they were rejecting me. After all that.

I thanked them for considering me. Then I called Tom. "Just wanted to check in," I said, trying not to sound as desperate as I was. My entire dream of starting a network of charter schools now depended on this seed funding from the Gates Foundation. "I was impressed with your business plan and I've passed it along to Bill Gates Sr.," he said. Thank God! I was relieved. "There's just one minor issue," he added. I held my breath. "We may have used up all our funds for this round. You may need to wait until next year. But don't worry, you'll be the first next year."

My heart sank, but there was no time to feel disappointed. I needed to see him in person to change his mind. "Do you have any plans to be in New York?" I asked. "Actually, I'm visiting a high school program run by Bard College in a few weeks," he said. "How about dinner?" I asked. "Sure. You pick the place."

In a month, I would know if my schools would become a reality or fall apart before they had even begun.

I called Bob at SUNY's Charter Schools Institute, our prospective authorizer, to check on the status of our application. His first question was whether I had received my funding. He reminded me that we would need to have it confirmed in time for the interview. "And I have some news for you," Bob said. "I'm leaving the Charter Schools Institute to join the governor's senior staff. Our general counsel, James Merriman, will be making the decision about whether to recommend you to the board." Charter approval in New York was based as much on the authorizer's evaluation of the leader as it was on the application. So I had to meet with James and make a very good impression. "Could we all get together?" I asked. "Sure," Bob said.

SUNY maintained offices in Albany and at One Penn Plaza in New York, near Madison Square Garden. Bob and James met me at their New York office the following week. James was now the key decision maker; even if I did get the money from Gates, his recommendation to the SUNY board would determine whether I'd be permitted to open schools. "She's relentless about learning," Bob said to

James. "You should have seen her at the NewSchools summit. She was like Don Shalvey's shadow. Whenever I turned around, middle of the day or middle of the night, there she was with a notebook, listening to Don, doing her homework." Thank goodness, I thought, at least this was going well. James told me that the charter interview would include several members of the SUNY board, including Ed Cox, cochair of SUNY's charter committee. "Ed was married in the Rose Garden of the White House," James told me. "His father-in-law was President Nixon." Great, no pressure or anything.

My interview date was approaching. It was imperative that I secure the funding commitment from Gates. Everything was riding on my dinner with Tom.

Outside, it was pouring rain, but I barely noticed that or the food as I spoke to Tom about the vision for the schools I so badly wanted to start. I explained that I couldn't wait for the following year and that I needed a letter with a funding commitment by May 2 in order to be approved for the charters. "It's just imperative that we start these schools," I said. In previous meetings, we had talked through every aspect of the business plan—the Jack Welch and Peter Drucker strategy, the financial and growth model, the facility plans, the Japanese approach to professional development. At this dinner, I decided to talk only about my vision. I spoke from my heart about Frankl, Kozol, and the vision to develop a "school for my children."

I offered Tom a ride to his hotel as I drove back to my home in Westchester. The hard rain had turned into a torrential downpour as I drove north on the FDR Drive, and the windshield wipers were not working. My father always got me old used cars, which meant there was always something broken. I couldn't see a thing and Tom told me to pull over. He jumped out of the car and did something to fix the wipers. When he got back in, he was soaking wet. "Oh my God! I'm so sorry," I said. "You're drenched!" He took it in stride. "Not to worry," he said. "I'm from Seattle. The rain doesn't bother me."

I reminded Tom yet again about the deadline for the letter, and prayed that he would come through. "I hear you," was all he said.

The day of the charter interview arrived before I knew it. And still no letter from the Gates Foundation. I had called Tom with a reminder just two days before. There was nothing more I could do.

I walked up the steps at Penn Plaza on Thursday morning for the interview, wearing the same black pants and sweater I had worn in California. The proposed school trustees met me there on the seventh floor. It was hard to project enthusiasm, since I was distracted by the lack of a financial commitment letter from the Gates Foundation. Tom knew that I needed it. He knew our charters were riding on it. And he knew that today was the big day.

I did everything in my power to force the funding out of my mind. It was showtime. Everyone had assembled around a huge oval conference table that took up the entire room. There was an empty seat at the head of the table and I was seated directly at the other end.

In walked the cochair of SUNY's charter committee, Ed Cox. Without even sitting down, he stood at the head of the table and fired away: "Nobody has ever asked for two charters at the same time. Why two?" I didn't have time to think—the words just popped into my head: "We want to change the world!" I blurted out. "We're not looking to start a school. We're looking to redefine school *systems*. So we have to start with more than one." I went on to explain my strategy of people, not product. The SUNY trustees asked a lot of smart, tough questions, and the prospective school board trustees all spoke. The interview was detailed and rigorous, but fair.

Before I knew it, the interview was over. James took me aside. "Your applications are outstanding. They are the best we've ever seen, and we want to recommend approval of both charters. But you realize, with no funding, there's nothing we can do." I told him I understood.

Just then, Gerry from the Charter Resource Center walked in; his offices were on the thirty-sixth floor in the same building. "A fax arrived to my office for you, Deborah," he said. Everyone stopped talking and stared at me—and the letter in Gerry's hand.

I said a prayer to myself as Gerry handed me the letter. "Good morning—and good news!" it said just below the Gates Foundation letterhead. "This is to inform you that you have been approved for a grant pending the approval of your two charters from the state authorizer." The noise in the room swelled, everyone was clapping and congratulating me. "Bravo!" Gerry said.

"How exciting," said James. Then, with his wry smile, he added, "Be careful what you wish for."

CHAPTER 7

STARTUP

I HAD BEEN WORKING FROM MY basement and commuting from Westchester into the city. When people canceled at the last minute—and it always seemed to happen on cold or rainy days—I'd be stuck looking for a coffee shop to work in for a few hours until the next meeting. I was nearing exhaustion and we hadn't even opened the school doors. What I really needed was an office in the city.

I didn't think it would be appropriate to pay for rent with the Gates funding. So I looked through the classifieds in *Crain's New York Business* for a rental office, and saw an ad for a company called Power-Space & Services. I called the main number and asked to speak with the manager. A woman named Kathy picked up the phone.

"Hi, my name is Deborah," I said. "You don't know me, but I'm starting a school in Harlem. I was hoping we could meet to discuss the possibility of donating office space because we don't have a school building yet." Kathy graciously invited me in and showed me around. Never before did I imagine that I'd be so excited about an office with phones and a copy machine. By the end of our discussion, Kathy said, "I'm going to provide you with donated space for the year. After September 11, if I can't help a fellow American . . ." and that was it. This woman who never met me before wanted to help.

Finally, with our Gates grant, we could pay startup salaries for a small team, including myself and a few others, who set up shop in that donated office on Madison Avenue and Forty-Fourth Street. There we methodically pushed through the hundreds of tasks that were now color-coded on a shared spreadsheet. We had to set up countless systems before the fall, so we read through hundreds of pages of material, and consulted with various experts to ensure we were in compliance and on track.

Our hundreds of small tasks could take anywhere from a few days to a few weeks each. Then there were major projects—like meeting with attorneys to understand student discipline laws, reviewing other schools' handbooks, and developing a draft of our policies—that could take even longer, sometimes months.

Andrew, who had played a key role in crafting the charter application, was filled with youthful energy and helped me with many other aspects of the startup. The two of us posted chart paper all over the office, on which we'd write lists of tasks for each week. When we brainstormed, more chart paper would go up. Soon it became impossible to see any of the actual wall. Our favorite word became "DONE!"—as in, "Done with the 7th Grade History Standards," "Done with the Employee Manual," or "Done ordering school supplies." Three tasks down, 997 to go. At one particularly giddy moment, Andrew yelled, "Done with the done!" which made us hysterical.

All this work took every ounce of our energy, and too many all-nighters fueled by more Coke and cookies than I cared to admit.

We were on a roll—or so I thought. I was under the impression that after completing our charter application and interview, along with numerous additional requirements like parent signatures and trustee background checks, the bureaucracy was behind us.

I was wrong.

Evidently, the State Education Department had the authority to submit their own set of questions, even though they were not our direct authorizer. One day I received an email with eighty-seven additional follow-up questions from someone at the State Education Department. Preparing this one document would require weeks at the computer—time that could have been spent getting ready to open the school. As I looked more closely at the questions, I realized that the education department saw our charter application as written in stone, and they planned to hold us to every detail. If the charter said the school day would end at 4:40, would we need to submit a revision if we wanted to change dismissal to 4:45? I called James, the new executive director of the Charter Schools Institute, right away.

"If I'm reading this correctly," I said to James, "the State Education Department plans to monitor us for compliance with this document rather than hold us accountable for results. Is that how it works?" If so, I explained to James, this would be a major problem. I planned to give enormous freedom to my teachers and team members. There was no way I'd hand them a charter with every aspect of the school spelled out.

I also knew from experience that nothing ever goes as planned. You try things out, but you have to take risks and make mistakes, then everything gets better over time. My fear was that the education department would sidetrack us with trivial questions about every minor detail. I worried they could require us to submit an endless stream of paperwork to revise the charter every time we wanted to make a change in our school.

Five years later I would experience just this type of bureaucratic nonsense when we sat in front of a panel for our charter renewal interview. The inspectors had visited for several days, interviewed all our teachers, observed classes, and asked us hundreds of questions. I was willing to be judged on performance and I understood the importance of such inspections to monitor school quality. But some of the questions were just plain silly. When one of the interviewers asked, in all seriousness, "We understand you run more than one school, but the students at each school may not. Do you consider it a problem that your logo says 'Harlem Village Academies'—plural?" I burst out laughing. Of course, I immediately realized that I might have just hurt our evaluation. I was reminded of one of my favorite scenes from the TV show *The West Wing*, when CJ, the White House press secretary, finds herself in the same situation and covers herself by saying, "Sorry, I just thought of something funny that happened with the deficit!" So I looked straight at the inspector and said with a straight face, "Sorry, I just thought of something funny that happened with the logo." After the meeting, we were all falling apart laughing at my complete inability to hide my disdain for bureaucracy.

The whole reason I wanted to start a charter was to be free from bureaucracy so we could focus on educating our students.

James totally got it. "Come to my office and bring your binders," he said.

I spent an entire day revising every aspect of the charters prior to their final approval. For every question and answer, I added words like *approximately, perhaps, draft,* and *preliminary.* It helped that James was a lawyer. But most of all, I appreciated that he understood how important this was to me. If I had to run interference for my future teachers, so be it. The bureaucrats could waste my time but I wasn't about to let them waste my teachers' time.

While we were making progress on educational plans, I was at step one—no, step zero—when it came to finding a school building.

Andrew and I headed to a national charter conference in Milwaukee, hoping to learn more about charter schools. While he attended a session on curriculum, the first workshop I walked into was packed full of charter school founders taking careful notes as the presenter outlined every aspect of developing a school building: the search process, acquisition, legal, financing, renovation, construction management, maintenance . . . it was overwhelming. I walked out after fifteen minutes, because I knew that the best use of my time would be to find someone who was an expert at real estate and ask for their help, rather than try to learn it myself. I met up with Andrew and told him that I was not qualified to develop a facility, and, more to the point, that taking a crash course made absolutely no sense. "Maybe they also have a workshop on how to become a dentist," I joked. "While you're there, I'll go to the workshop on brain surgery," he replied.

I still couldn't get over the fact that charter school students did not receive a school building. Soon Mayor Mike Bloomberg and Joel Klein would come on the scene in New York City and become the most transformative mayor and school chancellor in the country. Their visionary leadership was based on one simple premise: making decisions based on what's best for children. They would treat all children equally by providing charter school students—who were, after all, public school students—with facility space. But all that hadn't happened yet. So we were forced to spend precious time and money figuring out how to secure our own school building.

Luckily I discovered Civic Builders, a new organization that specialized in charter school facility development. Annie Tirschwell, Civic's cofounder and I, searched for space for six months in East Harlem, Central Harlem, and West Harlem. We had looked at everything from empty parking lots to abandoned offices to church basements, but nothing was feasible or affordable. We would talk on the phone at precisely 7:10 a.m. each day—as I walked or, more often than not, ran, from my car to the train—to check in with each other about updates and next steps. (I always scheduled calls during travel time like this. As a single mom I needed to use every minute efficiently.)

Then, one Friday afternoon, Annie called my cell phone. "You've got to meet me in East Harlem!" she said.

"Okay, but I'm in a cab on my way across town to interview an accountant," I explained. "How about in two hours?" Annie insisted that it had to be immediately.

"You may have no school for the bookkeeper to manage if you don't have a building! This is the one needle in the haystack. It's a perfect space. But they have a few offers and they're making a decision today. Deborah, you have got to get your butt up here." I called the accountant to apologize and asked the cabbie to turn around and head east toward First Avenue.

When I got out at 120th Street, I saw right away why Annie was so adamant. It was perfect: an old public school building that had been converted into a community center. The building was right next to a public housing project.

Annie was waiting for me in the lobby. We went upstairs to see the space—the whole second floor. The director of the East Harlem Council for Community Improvement, which oversaw the building, told us he had several offers from other organizations, including another charter. I spoke with him about our vision and plans, and all the ways we'd be a good tenant. After he had met with us for an hour, we had a deal.

The space needed new electrical wiring, tiles, paint, and many other renovations, but at least it had walls, doors, and windows—a major improvement over most of the other spaces we had seen. Next task: finding a contractor.

Despite the infinite amount of operational tasks, I was determined to spend as much time as possible visiting excellent schools. There was no such thing as a charter school startup training in New York so I had to put together a training for myself. I compiled a list of the best charter, private, and district public schools in the Northeast, and I proceeded to conduct field research: visiting dozens of schools, meeting with principals, observing instruction, and asking hundreds of questions.

South Boston Harbor Academy was famous for being at the top of the charts for student achievement, and the school's founder, Brett Peiser, had an exceptional reputation. During my first visit I noticed that he was soft-spoken, smart, and humble.

Brett talked with me at great length and in great detail about the practical challenges of opening and leading a school. I was interested in every aspect of the school day, from academics and arts, to his bathroom break system, after-school clubs, and homework folders. I was so impressed with him that I asked if we could meet again, and to my surprise, Brett offered to meet weekly for four months while I developed my new school. Given how much I had learned in just one day, and how many questions I still had (for each question, I had at least five follow-ups), I immediately took him up on the offer.

At 2:15 that first day Brett asked if I was hungry. "A little," I said, assuming we would go to a nearby diner. Instead, we walked three steps out of his school to an outdoor food cart, where he purchased a banana and a Diet Coke. "Just like Don Shalvey!" I exclaimed. "Though at least you're having a banana instead of potato chips. Do charter school leaders ever eat?" Brett laughed. "Not during the school day," he said. "We're too busy." I loved these people!

Eventually we did eat. That night, Brett and I had dinner with a good friend of his, whose school I had also visited. I asked so many follow-up questions that they started making fun of me. But it was all in good cheer. I felt immensely grateful to the charter leaders who so generously shared all their knowledge with me during my startup period.

I was becoming accustomed to what I would see in high-performing charters: energetic teachers, disciplined students, and incredibly smart, driven school leaders.

I remember walking into a fifth-grade phonics lesson with Doug McCurry, cofounder of Amistad Academy in New Haven, Connecticut. "Follow along with your fingers. The word is blast. B-L-A-S-T," said the teacher. "What word?!" Without missing a beat the children responded in unison, "Blast!"

This school was finally teaching these children what their prior schools had failed to do year after year. But the injustice was appalling. The fifth graders were learning the sounds of letters—something that the children of the Yale professors nearby had learned in kindergarten.

Back in New York, everyone suggested I meet Kristin Kearns Jordan, founder of Bronx Prep. Her school was only in its second year of operation but she was considered an expert because it was one of only a few charter schools that existed in the city. "Do you have a detailed budget yet?" she asked. "Yes and no," I replied. "What do you mean?" I explained that I considered our budget—and all aspects of our schools—to be a work in progress until I recruited the founding teachers. "It's hard to know exactly how much we'll spend as I don't yet know which books the teachers will want to buy," I said.

She looked skeptical. "That may not be practical," she said. "If teachers select their own curriculum, you could end up wasting a lot of money. How can you order different kinds of books every time you hire a new teacher?" It was a good point and one I hadn't fully considered. Now I was worried, but I was still determined to give the teachers the power to make these decisions. I marked it down in my notebook as something I'd have to figure out later.

Kristin took me on a tour of her school, where kids met in trailers because she had already outgrown her temporary facility. "It's not easy," she told me, "but we do whatever we have to do for the kids." That was the pervasive attitude in the charter community.

In one late-night email exchange, Amistad Academy's Doug McCurry started a note to me and a few other charter leaders with "Dear Charter Maniacs." I loved the energy and the entrepreneurial spirit among these education reformers. Linda Brown, founder of the Building Excellent Schools program, would later tell an audience that you know a true charter school leader when you email them on Memorial Day weekend and get a reply within five minutes.

But the most important thing I learned after several months of observing was that each school did things differently. Some high-performing charter schools made extensive use of data, while others did not. Some school leaders believed that summer school was critical to student success, and others thought the summer should be used for teacher development. Though my study of effective schools was statistically insignificant, I felt sure of my conclusion. "There is only one common element of excellent schools," I wrote in my notebook. "Talented people who are exceptionally motivated. How do you replicate *people*?"

CHAPTER 8

ROCK STARS

I STARTED INTERVIEWING TEACHERS, and in time I'd meet hundreds and hundreds of them. Soon I would discover that they almost all felt the same: frustrated with their schools and with the public school system. "The principal is managing an assembly line and teachers are expected to keep the machine running," one teacher told me. "It's a joke. They don't care what I'm doing." Their emotions ran from mild discouragement to exasperation.

Our school had to become the place that we had described in the business plan—the best place to work on the planet. I wanted to create a nirvana for teachers that would attract the best and brightest to join us.

Creating that nirvana turned out to be much harder than I expected.

To me, teaching was not a job, it was a sacred mission—and I wanted to hire people who felt the same way. People who loved children, cared deeply about instructional quality, and who would never dream of rushing out the door at 2:45. No clock-punchers. Period.

I wanted everyone on the team to share a fierce urgency for erad-icating educational inequity. I wanted to go to work every day with people who would see a problem and figure out how to solve it with-out even being asked.

There was one issue that concerned me: accountability. The anti–accountability outlook was pervasive in public education. So many educators believed results were ultimately not within their control because of outside factors like poverty, or lack of parental support.

The charter community had the opposite attitude, which could be summed up in three words: whatever it takes. It was a school's job to do whatever it takes to ensure a child's success. This outlook unified charter school leaders, and it seemed so obvious and right.

Accountability was a practical matter as well. The charter could be taken away at any time if we did not perform well on state tests.

Ultimately, I was looking for teachers who shared my nuanced view: we had to hold ourselves personally accountable to knock the ball out of the park on the state tests, even as we understood that the most important things educators impart to students can't be measured by standardized exams. The way I saw it, if you provided a high level education, then performing well on tests would become a by-product. You did not need to teach to the test. You could teach above it. "The test is an inanimate object," I used to joke. "It is not forcing us to teach to it."

It would be a challenge to find teachers who shared my vision for higher-level learning and were also willing to be held accountable for test results—so much so that they'd be willing to give up the job pro-tection of the union to join our team. "If a candidate derides testing, run the other way," one education reform friend advised. "Watch out for the granola-kumbaya-poetry-loving teacher," another joked. "Wait a minute," I said, "that sounds like me!"

In the fall of 2002, Teachers College was holding a job fair and I had just hired a Teach For America alum as a part-time recruiter. We made a poster, designed a brochure, bought an easel, and piled all our supplies into my car. I arrived on campus at Broadway and 120th Street, my old stomping grounds, at 7:30 a.m. on Saturday. For six hours we talked with prospective teachers. By the next day we had set up interviews with the best of the bunch.

If an interview went well I made an appointment to see the potential teacher in action. The problem was that we did not have a school building to hold model lessons. So I trekked all over the five boroughs—sometimes from Brooklyn to the South Bronx in one day—watching teachers in their classrooms.

The first teacher I visited had a spectacular résumé. She had come across during the interview as smart and caring. When I arrived at her high school, it was 10:30 a.m. Out front, I noticed something strange: cars filled with teenage boys would speed toward the school, stop in front for a second while a few more boys came out of the school building and jumped in, and then they would race away. I asked a police officer standing outside what was going on. "Every day, ma'am," he said, shaking his head. "What exactly are they doing?" I asked. "The gangs drive by, kids they just swipe and leave," he answered. "What do you mean, 'swipe and leave'?" I asked. "They swipe their ID so they get credit for being in school, then as soon as they can sneak out of class, they leave the building and go off with their friends."

I stood there for another ten minutes watching dozens of kids laughing as they jumped into cars that were speeding by. "Why do they even bother to show up to school, then?" I asked. "For the breakfast and free MetroCards," he explained. "And why do you suppose the school allows that?" But before the officer could answer, I got it. "They need to make their attendance and graduation numbers."

I walked into the building, past five more policemen, and found my way to room 340. When I slipped in the door, the teacher smiled excitedly and invited me to sit in the back. Fifteen students were in her ninth-grade history class, of whom six were listening to music on headphones.

About ten seconds after I sat down, a teenage boy threw a pencil at the blackboard and the other kids snickered. Not three minutes later, one boy announced that he needed a tissue and walked out the door. Another boy said, "Me, too," and followed after him. The other kids looked at each other sneering. Neither of them returned in the forty-five minutes I was there. Almost all the boys were slouching, with the hoods of their sweatshirts pulled over their heads, and most of the girls were dressed promiscuously. One student had written "Fuck History" on the spine of his binder. For a split second I thought it was funny. I had rebelled against the establishment myself, and I'd raised my kids to question authority. But this young man was not an informed skeptic, as the great Ted Sizer would say. He was just missing out on what should have been his education. The teacher had absolutely no control of the class, despite her intelligence and dedication.

While it was obvious within five minutes that she was not going to be teaching in my school, I stayed for the full class period, both to be polite and also because I was fascinated with what I was seeing. Toward the end of the lesson, the teacher announced that the students would be taking a quiz in groups. Huh? "There will be extra credit for cooperative learning," she said. What a pitiful interpretation of the concept of cooperative learning. I imagined it was this kind of poor execution of progressive educational methods that caused the conservatives' back-to-basics backlash.

The following week, I visited a veteran educator in the South Bronx who was interviewing for the position of dean. He had been a dean in the school I was visiting and had been promoted to assistant principal. When I arrived, he had a full tour planned. We walked into classrooms where the students seemed to be behaving and learning.

Then he took us into a room where four teachers were trying to review data to inform their instruction, though their conclusions were not particularly astute.

As he guided us carefully through certain halls—entering some rooms and bypassing others—I realized I was getting the VIP tour. So I quietly slipped away from the group and quickly walked down the hall. I was looking for the cafeteria: That's where I'd see the real behavior of students in his school.

When I walked down the dingy stairway into the cafeteria, three policewomen were standing in a corner near the lunch trays, chatting with each other and eating salad. Farther inside, students were screaming, jumping, and running wild all over. There was a lunch monitor blowing a whistle, but the students were ignoring her.

Far back in the right corner I saw a group of students gathered around a cafeteria table. A boy and girl stood on top of the table explicitly simulating various sex acts. Kids laughed as they watched. An adult sat on a chair, observing the whole thing. I walked over to him. "Are they allowed to do that?" I asked, knowing it was a ridiculous question. Why was he taking no responsibility for the students' behavior? He did not answer me or even look at me, but he stood up and yelled at them, which the students completely ignored. Then he sat back down with a look on his face that told me to mind my own business.

The assistant principal ran over to me, practically out of breath. "What are you doing?" he asked. "One of the security guards radioed me that you're here. Please, let's go back upstairs." I looked back at the students. "Sorry about that," I said to him.

I was hoping for more luck the next week. I had an interview with a teacher from Los Angeles who had seen our online advertisement and sent us a letter of interest and four glowing references. His résumé was impressive and I was excited to meet him. I would not be able to see him teach, since he was flying in from the west coast to meet me and visit several other schools, so he had sent a full lesson on video. I watched the video at home, and it was spectacular. His students were well behaved, his lesson was interesting, and he clearly knew his subject matter. He made learning fun for those kids——you could see in their eyes how much they were enjoying it. Finally! I couldn't wait to meet him.

When he arrived at our midtown office, he brought a portfolio with samples of student work, his lesson plans, testimonials from his students, and data that demonstrated outstanding academic achievement gains. His presentation was colorful, professional, and organized. It was clear that the references were right: He was charismatic, and his students loved him.

But the more we spoke, the more clearly I could see there was a problem. This teacher talked too much about how great he was. I knew his arrogance would drive his colleagues crazy.

The next week I interviewed a teacher who seemed to have many great qualities: warmth, intelligence, and humility. I invited her to take the next step in the process: I would observe her teaching a writing lesson in her school.

When I arrived, her fourth-grade students were in the middle of writing in black and white marble notebooks, and the desks were organized into six groups of three. The classroom was decorated beautifully with colorful posters, mobiles hanging from the ceiling, charts and artwork everywhere. It felt like a nurturing environment. I was hopeful.

The boys and girls seemed to be enjoying themselves. Their task had something to do with writing a personal narrative, although I could not yet figure out what they were supposed to be learning. They were talking to each other in groups.

A few minutes into the lesson, the teacher asked for quiet, but the children ignored her. She clapped her hands in a rhythm and three students responded with the same clap, while the fifteen others ignored her. Then she yelled, "This is unacceptable, boys and girls! I will wait for you to be quiet!" which got about three more kids' attention. "I'm still waiting," she said. I never understood that phrase—why would teachers admit out loud that they were waiting? It was an admission that they were unable to command the students' attention. She looked at me and I smiled, feeling sorry for her, and trying to show support with my eyes. It was painful to watch, as she meant well but could not control a room full of nine-year-olds.

"Look at table two!" she exclaimed. "They get a point because they are all quiet." I looked carefully at the reactions of the other students. Many of the children rolled their eyes as if to say, "I'm nine, I don't care about points," and a few who had previously been quiet now started talking again. This tactic had only seemed to make things worse. "I like how Brianna is paying attention," she said, her tone now sounding a bit desperate as the children continued to ignore her. "Okay, that's it! I'm going to start giving out check marks to anyone who is still talking, and those with three checks will miss recess," she threatened. The students did not seem to care a whit. Perhaps they did not believe her.

"Could we finish the story from yesterday?" a little girl yelled loudly, without raising her hand. "Only if everyone is quiet," the teacher yelled back. It must have been a good story because the children were suddenly all quiet. She had given up trying to teach that day's lesson. Instead, she started reading from *Runaway Ralph*, by Beverly Cleary and the children were instantly happy.

After reading aloud for about three minutes, she looked around at their beautiful, innocent faces. "I want you to fall in love with reading," she said sweetly. "That's why I'm sharing my favorite book with you." The students continued to listen quietly for more than six minutes. Her voice was soothing and the class was calm. Yes, she had trouble commanding authority. But this teacher was bright and kind, and really loved the students.

Suddenly a large woman in a bright orange dress with a big silver necklace walked in and stood in the front doorway. "That's the principal," a little boy whispered to me. "GOOD MORNING!" she said in a booming voice. The teacher ignored the principal, looked at me, rolled her eyes in exasperation, and tried to keep reading the story to the kids. She had just spent almost ten minutes getting them quiet and attentive, and they were immersed in listening to the book she was reading aloud. "I *said*—good *morning*, class," bellowed the principal, derailing the little bit of contentment the teacher had established. I was incredulous, but the students seemed to be used to this type of interruption. This time the children responded, "Good morning," at which point the principal promptly walked away. A few girls started giggling and mumbling and within a half minute, the class was out of the teacher's control again.

Finally, she gave up. "You will have some free play time until the end of the period," the teacher said. That would be twenty minutes of free play. She had the best intentions, and I felt sympathy for the lack of support this teacher was getting in her school. But I didn't hire her.

"We just struck gold!" our recruiter Jenny said. "You have got to meet this teacher, Deborah. She's in Dorchester, Massachusetts, now, but she's moving to New York to live with her boyfriend. My contacts say she's supposed to be amazing." I lit up: it was always exciting to hear about a rock star candidate.

Her name was Rebecca. She had been a teacher for six years. I went to Boston to meet with her, and as we started talking, I noticed a few things right off the bat: Rebecca was smart, sincere, and intensely modest. She reminded me of my Gates Foundation friends, with her bohemian style and sophisticated intellect.

Jenny had told Rebecca about my concerns with accountability, so Rebecca came prepared. She brought a binder filled with charts that demonstrated the reading comprehension gains made by each of her students. Despite her mild manner, she spoke confidently about her approach to teaching reading. She clearly knew so much more about literacy than I did.

Rebecca was the type of teacher I was hoping to find. We arranged a date for me to observe her teach a lesson.

When I arrived at the public school where Rebecca taught fifth grade, I was still nervous. I was so new at evaluating prospective teaching candidates. So I invited a friend, a charter school leader from Boston, to join me to provide a second, more informed, opinion.

The school bell was ringing loudly outside when we arrived. As we walked toward the front stairs, a student was throwing a tantrum. A teacher was yelling at him as he sat on the blacktop, refusing to get up. She stopped for a moment to smile at us politely and say good morning, then continued yelling as I opened the large door and walked inside.

After signing in with security, we ascended the huge stairway up five flights. We had arrived early, so I walked slowly, taking in the surroundings. On every floor, teachers were shouting, and students were yelling over them as they ran around the halls and darted in and out of classrooms. When I hit the third floor, the bell rang loudly and I heard an adult shout at the top of her lungs, "First period. Sit down *now!*" The bedlam in the third-floor hallway proceeded nonetheless.

The first-period bell also didn't faze the students who were still running around a few minutes later when we finally got to the fifth floor. It was still relative chaos in the halls. We walked toward Rebecca's room, and opened the door.

Just like that, we entered another realm. It was calm and quiet. I felt like I had entered a magical fairyland, with beautiful student artwork hanging from the ceiling, charts with literary terms, colorful posters, folders with student names printed neatly. Everything was so beautiful and so organized. And the books! Rebecca's room had three different types of bookshelves, and on top of that, there were books displayed everywhere in the room, covering every possible surface: books on windowsills, books on the chalk trays of blackboards, books on top of cabinets, books absolutely everywhere! This was a classroom where I would want my own children.

Even after we opened the rickety door, the students did not look at us—they were intently focused on their writing. The desks were arranged in cooperative learning clusters: four groups of five and two groups of four, and every single one of Rebecca's students was seated and working.

It was a wonderful sight, but I had to wonder whether Rebecca had the gifted class. There was no other explanation. Our school would not have the luxury that this school had—or so it appeared—to select the highest-level students and put them in one classroom. Our students would come in by open, public lottery, most of them three to four years or more behind grade level. Teaching in a charter school would be much harder than cherry-picking the best students. How would I be able to extrapolate from this whether she'd be up to the challenge?

Rebecca sat at a small table in the corner, conferencing with five students. As she got up from the table and walked over to us, I noticed that she was wearing rainbow-colored, flowered tights with a contrasting patterned skirt, and bright clogs. "Hi," Rebecca said, smiling. She handed each of us a copy of her four-page typed lesson plan, with the words "Poetry Workshop" printed on top, and quickly went back to the students at the small conference table.

I receded into the opposite corner of the room for a few minutes and looked at the lesson plan. It was not the type of lesson that I had observed at most high-performing charter schools. The lesson plan she had designed called for students to analyze a classic poem and then write an original poem using a similar literary device or theme.

As I walked around the classroom, I saw that the students were compiling a poetry anthology with copies of both poems—the model and their own. Students were engaging in a close reading and highly sophisticated analysis of text that was very far from the test-prep curriculum I had seen in so many other urban schools. "This is the type of English instruction I've been dreaming of," I whispered to my friend. "This is it—this is my vision!"

But would this type of lesson be effective for students who lacked basic reading skills? I just didn't know. I'd have to follow my gut.

About six minutes into the lesson, the students were still happily writing—still not a peep from anyone. Suddenly a boy wearing a short-sleeved shirt that was about two sizes too small stood up without raising his hand. Here we go, I thought. The perfect behavior was bound to end at some point. Rebecca glanced at him for a split second but didn't say anything. He walked away from his group quietly toward a short bluish-green wood cabinet, and opened the door. Inside there were small word-processing keyboards. He took one, closed the door gently, went back to his seat, and began to type his poem. I was spellbound. A few minutes later, other children did the same, and each time, the rest of the students did not look up from their own work when their classmate went to the cabinet. The first boy then got up again. He walked to the other side of the room, plugged the word processor into a printer, and smiled proudly as he printed out his poem. A few other students who seemed to be finished writing had taken out poetry books from under their desks and started reading. This self-directed behavior was exquisite.

Although she was quite young, Rebecca reminded me of Ms. Savarese, the second-grade teacher in Dobbs Ferry who had taught my three children. In fact, Ms. Savarese was one of the reasons we moved to Westchester. When Joel and I had first visited schools when the kids were very young, we observed her class and spoke with her at length afterward. We were very impressed. Years later, Ms. Savarese retired and moved to Martha's Vineyard, and I took the kids to visit her. She was, to me, the ideal American teacher: she took immense pride in teaching second grade for more than twenty years, and my children were the beneficiaries of her wisdom and expertise. Ms. Savarese was the symbol in my mind of what I hoped all our teachers would aspire to: a lifetime in the classroom.

A few more minutes went by and Rebecca stood up. "Okay, everyone, please stop what you are doing and come and join me on the rug."

Every single child followed her instructions immediately. They tucked their chairs under their desks and walked expeditiously to the rug in the corner. Within thirty seconds, the entire class was seated cross-legged on the carpet, in a perfect U, facing Rebecca, without one student so much as bumping into another. Rebecca sat in the middle and held a book of poetry outward so the children could look at the cover. One boy started fidgeting ever so slightly and blocked the view of two classmates. "Scoot back, John," Rebecca said. The entire class was silent for about two seconds while he did not follow the instruction. Rebecca continued to hold up the book facing the rest of the class so they could look at the cover while she looked straight at John with a gravely serious face. She lowered her voice to a faint whisper, "Scoot back—now." He quickly did, and she broke into a big smile and began reading *Honey, I Love*, by Eloise Greenfield.

Her hour-long lesson had flown by, and I didn't want to leave. But I was due for a school visit in Roxbury. As we walked out, my friend asked me what I thought. "I love her! And I loved the poetry analysis. The lesson was amazing: she is the kind of teacher I would want for my own children. What do you think?"

"I agree," my friend said. "She's smart. But you should probe her about her attitude on testing and accountability."

By the time I got back to New York the next day, the recruiter Jenny had confirmed that Rebecca's class was not made up of gifted students. Indeed, they were a random selection of students. "Okay, I'm going to call her tonight," I said.

It was 7:30 p.m. and my kids were doing their homework. I went upstairs to my bedroom to call Rebecca. She said that she had told her boyfriend that she wanted to join our team. I told her how much I loved her lesson and that I had just a few questions. I asked her again about testing and teacher accountability. "What more can I say to convince you that I'm willing to be accountable for results?" she replied politely. Then I asked my last question. "What makes you want to work for us, specifically?" Rebecca didn't hesitate for a moment. "It's the vision," she said. "You're doing the school that nobody thinks can be done."

I had been in dozens of urban classrooms by now, and I saw the same approach to teaching math everywhere I went. Teachers used chants and games and drills to make math fun, and a seemingly endless supply of rap songs and tricks for memorizing formulas. At first I had been really taken with it all. When you compare this level of engagement to the boredom and failure in urban schools, you can't help but be impressed. But when I asked myself the only question that mattered—would I want my own kids to learn this way?—I had to be honest. No, I would not. I didn't want my kids to "learn" math by memorizing tricks. I wanted them to grapple with problems and to think deeply about how to figure out solutions by doing the hard work for themselves. I wanted them to fall in love with math itself: to be enchanted with the challenge of mastering difficult math concepts, not with a song that helped them memorize a formula. I was looking for a founding math teacher who shared and embodied this vision—a teacher in whose classroom I would happily put my own kids. I found that when I met Nick.

When Nick and I met for an initial interview in my midtown office space, we connected immediately over *The Teaching Gap*, a book we both loved that described the differences in teaching methods in Japan, Germany, and the United States. *The Teaching Gap* also described a Japanese approach to professional development called lesson study, in which teachers plan a lesson together, observe each other teaching, and then discuss feedback to improve the lesson. Nick had actually taken part in a lesson study group in Paterson, New Jersey.

Nick was soft-spoken and thoroughly professional. We talked about our shared enthusiasm for lesson study. Within an hour we were completing each other's sentences. Nick lit up when he heard that lesson study would be part of the new school system I was starting.

And we really connected about our shared passion for sophisticated instruction. Most of the teachers I had observed explained math procedures while students listened (they called this "I do"), followed by a sample problem ("we do"), then independent student practice ("you do"). I was not particularly impressed—even if they livened it up with songs—because this shallow method essentially provided students with the conclusion at the beginning of the lesson. Instead, I wanted our students to grapple with problems, as they did in Singapore and Japan. I wanted each student to actually construct the solution with careful guidance from the teacher. In other words, the teacher should not be doing the majority of the work; the students should be doing the thinking and working. And I felt this way about every subject, not just math. In fact, I felt so strongly about this that we had emphatically stated it in the charter application—"the students should do the intellectual heavy lifting"—and it would become our mantra for years ahead.

"The teacher should be a coach who walks around the room and watches what the kids are doing on their own," Nick said. "Then he uses that information to help the class break through their struggles." Exactly! I had to restrain myself from offering him a job on the spot.

It would be a long shot to convince Nick to join our team. He was a family man who had come to teaching as a second career and he had three children to support who would soon be approaching college age.

He would be giving up not only tenure at his public school, but also a pension, to work in a school that did not yet exist. The other problem was New York City: Nick was not particularly excited about a long commute on top of a longer school day.

Before I knew it, ninety minutes had gone by. I asked Nick if he would be open to my observing him teach the following week. "Sure," he said.

I drove from Westchester to Paterson early the next week. Nick's classroom could not have been more different from Rebecca's. The walls were bare. There was not a single thing on the walls—not a thing! Not even a poster. It was just Nick, his chalk, and his passion for math.

"The blackboard is a story board," Nick would later tell me, "and I use it very strategically. Every single thing that goes on the blackboard is in a particular place for a particular reason." He didn't want kids focused on anything else on the walls.

On this day Nick started his lesson by giving each student a piece of graph paper. The only thing on the paper was a triangle. His instruction: find the area of the inside of the triangle.

How could these students possibly approach the problem on their own? There was no obvious way to solve the problem. Most of the kids started counting the squares inside the triangle, just as they had done for the rectangle the day before. But today they got confused, because some of the little squares on the graph paper were cut through the middle by the line of the triangle.

A few of the students were becoming a bit frustrated, but you could see they were still trying. Nick walked around the room and watched but he did not help them. He let them struggle. I was mesmerized by his teaching method. But I was even more fascinated with his calm and confidence. It was almost as if he knew exactly what was going to happen.

Nick would tell me afterward that he knew what they would do when he gave them the problem, because he had taught this lesson in the past, and he had refined the lesson based on his prior experience teaching it.

Just as Nick expected, some kids counted the squares inside the triangle since that's what they had done the day before for rectangles. Other kids tried to find the area of the triangle by using the method they had learned to find the area of a rectangle the day before: multiplying the base times the height. Nick knew that neither of these approaches would work, and neither was correct. He let them do it anyway. Nick didn't need songs to help him "make math interesting" or fun, because he made the math itself interesting. *Exactly* what I would want for my own kids, I thought. He didn't need tricks to help students memorize anything, because they were figuring out the underlying concepts themselves, so they would easily remember the formula. After a few minutes, he called the class to attention.

"Let's compare the number you got when you counted the squares to what you got when you multiplied the base by the height."

Nick did not ask for random volunteers. Instead, he purposefully called on particular students by name. "Judith, what was your answer, and which method did you use?" He later told me that he asked specific students based on his prior circulating around the room and seeing what they were doing, so that he would have a variety of answers for the class discussion.

"I counted the squares. I got 12," Judith answered. "*Exactly* 12?" Nick asked. "Well, some of the squares were cut off by the triangle so it was *about* 12."

"How many other students used the 'counting the squares' method?" Nick asked.

About half the class raised their hands and Nick asked them to call out how many squares they had counted. One said 11, another said 10, another said 12 just like Judith, and a fifth kid said 13.

As they all spoke, Nick wrote their numbers—12, 11, 10, 12, 13—

on the left side of a T-chart on the board, then "Counting the Squares Method" on top. The kids were paying close attention to what he was writing—I noticed that they were completely engaged and following every step.

Nick was smiling as he asked the next question. Again he called on a particular student while knowing in advance (because he had looked at each kid's paper while they were working independently) what that student would say. "Harvier, what method did you use?" and the student answered, "I multiplied the two sides of the triangle." Nick wrote on the board: "multiplying the sides of the right angle."

"And what number did you get?" Nick asked. "Twenty-four," replied Harvier, as Nick wrote down "24" on the board on the right column.

Then Nick asked four other students who had used the "multiplying the sides" method what answer they got, and all of them said the same exact number: 24. Nick wrote their answers on the board after Harvier's answer: 24, 24, 24, 24, 24.

At this point, every student was focused on the board. Some were confused, some were slightly frustrated, but they were all consumed by the math. I was in love with this lesson. And I was dreaming of our schools filled with students falling in love with math.

Nick became just slightly theatrical. He stared at the board as if he were confused!

"I want you to stare at these numbers for thirty seconds and *think*. What questions do you have? There's no talking, no raising hands. Look at the numbers for thirty seconds. Just *think*."

The room was dead silent. In all the schools I had visited, I had never before seen an entire classroom of students this absorbed in a math problem.

Then Nick said, "Okay, talk to your neighbor!" and the room erupted in a boisterous discussion about triangles. I listened in to the discussion. Every kid in that classroom was talking about the math problem; not a single one was interested in chatting about what was on TV the night before.

The students were excited, as they had discovered that all the numbers on the left side were about half of the number 24 on the right side. But that's all they knew at that point. They still did not know how to calculate the area of a triangle.

Nick asked, "Is one of these answers the area of the triangle? Are they both right? Are neither right? We don't know. The one thing we've discovered is this . . ." The suspense Nick generated reminded me a bit of Mel Reisfeld and his feigned theatrics when lecturing about history. Then Nick wrote on the board: "The area we got by counting the squares was about half the area we got by multiplying the legs of the right angle."

Nick would later explain to me the significance of the statement he was writing on the board. In every lesson in Japan there is one big statement that is pivotal to the lesson, and it goes on the board. That statement is not the formula: It's the concept underlying the formula. It's the "why" or "how"—and if a student can understand that big idea, they will understand how to solve the particular problem.

"It's interesting, isn't it?" he said, "Okay, now I have another problem for you to solve."

The students protested. "Wait! We didn't finish!"

This was a typical district public school. These were the students whom so many in the education establishment wrote off as unable to learn because of "the conditions of poverty," yet here they were—every one of them—dying to understand this math concept. A passionate teacher made them passionate about learning.

"We want to finish the first problem!" Nick smiled and said, "I know but I have another problem I need you to work on."

He gave them another piece of graph paper. The anticipation of what would happen next was giving me butterflies. Not being a math person, I am embarrassed to admit, I didn't know. On the paper there was a rectangle with a diagonal line inside the rectangle going from the top right corner to the bottom left corner, such that there were two triangles inside the rectangle. The triangle on the right was shaded gray and the triangle on the left was filled with the graph paper boxes.

I looked over the shoulder of a student in the back and saw the instructions that Nick had written on the paper: "Find the area of the shaded triangle."

Within a few seconds, as the students started reading the instructions and looking at the two triangles inside the rectangle, one student after another started exclaiming "Ooooohhhhh!" and "I get it!" and "Oh my God!" I got it too—and I was just as excited.

Nick was amazing. I would have happily put my three kids in his classroom all year, just as I would have in Rebecca's. That was my criterion for hiring teachers.

We chatted after his lesson, and Nick knew that I'd be making an offer. He told me he'd been thinking about it nonstop. He had spoken with his wife and colleagues. It was a big decision.

When he accepted, I was thrilled.

I had spent almost a year searching for rock stars—master teachers to anchor our new school—and I had found them in Nick and Rebecca. But something bothered me: finding such great teachers for every classroom in the country did not seem scalable. If the key to fixing public education was to find millions of rock stars, we were all doomed. Now I was even more obsessed by the question: How do you give every child in America an excellent teacher?

CHAPTER 9

THE PATH TO JUSTICE

"DO YOU HAVE A CHILD IN fourth grade?" Yohana asked passersby on the sidewalk of 125th Street as she handed out flyers about our new school. I had hired her in February to help recruit students, and she was tireless—chatting up parents at supermarkets, schools, and housing projects. Yohana was cheerful and bubbly, and people responded to her.

I'd met Yohana at Edison along with Diallo, another part-timer I'd hired. He was an enterprising fellow, tall, thin, and brimming with energy. They were both willing to take on multiple jobs, which was precisely what I needed on our startup team.

Yohana flagged down parents with young children at bus stops and didn't hesitate to walk up to mothers in the vegetable aisle. Diallo and I met with parents as well, in church basements and Harlem community centers. Almost without exception, the parents we met were frustrated with their local schools.

"My son's school is out of control," one mother with a black coat, bright red hat, red scarf, and red high-heeled boots told me outside near the Abyssinian Baptist Church on Frederick Douglass Boulevard. After talking for five minutes, she was interested. "The school on our block is filthy," she said. "And it's dirty and disgusting!" added her little boy, practically jumping up to participate in our conversation. Her name was Grace and her son, a short boy with glasses, was Kareem. I later learned that he had good grades, loved chess, and had never met his father. His father had been in jail since Kareem was little. "Every day there are fights," Grace sighed. I asked Kareem what he does when he sees a fight. "I don't know what to do. If I stand there I get kicked in the face. But if I run away, the other kids call me a loser." As he spoke I saw Grace tearing up. I prayed he would make it into the lottery.

Our simple, one-page application asked for a name, contact info, and Social Security number. There were no admission requirements, no transcript or behavior background checks, and no interviews.

Once parents understood that we really did have open admissions—the lottery was monitored by auditors, and there was no way for us to select the top applicants—many opened up about their children. "He's getting F's and D's, and a few C's," a young mother confided to Diallo at a bus stop on Lenox Avenue. Her son Brandon was a fourth grader at a local public school. The year before, he and a bunch of third-grade boys had thrown pencils at each other and the teacher had walked out of the room. The incident had escalated into a full-blown fight and Brandon came home with slashes near his eye.

At first I had been worried about whether we'd be able to recruit students for a school that didn't yet exist, that didn't have a building, that lacked a complete faculty, and was called a "charter school," a concept completely unknown at the time to most parents.

As it turned out, it was easy to get families to sign up. The situation in Harlem public schools was desperate. We heard the same themes from most of the children: The teacher yells. The teacher doesn't care if we're late. Nobody checks my work. Nobody helps me. The kids laugh at me. The kids are mean to me. School is boring. School is a waste of time.

And the most common theme—what we heard over and over from fourth graders—was the constant fighting. "There are so many bullies," said one girl. "I don't want to get in a fight," said another, "so sometimes I eat lunch in the bathroom."

Parents were thrilled when we told them about our plans for a longer school day, Saturday tutoring, and strict discipline. But what they really responded to was our emphasis on accountability. When a mother at one of our information sessions heard me say that the teachers and I would hold ourselves personally responsible for the quality of their child's education, she called out "You go girl!" The room broke out in smiles. But then she went on, "Our school is horrible. And there are grown men lurking around. But there's nothing I can do. I can't control where I live." All the mothers nodded.

At another session, when I asked the group if they had any questions, one grandmother leaped out of her seat and said, "Yes, I have just one. Where do I sign up?!" Everyone laughed. But when I spoke with her after the presentation, I learned that her grandchild's situation was anything but funny. She told me that she was taking care of her granddaughter Jasmine because she had been abandoned by her mother, a recovering alcoholic who had been abused by her husband. Two of Jasmine's four sisters, ages fourteen and fifteen, had babies of their own. Jasmine was great in math but had failed reading in third grade and was struggling again this year. But what really upset me was what their elementary school principal had told her grandmother. "He told me that I should not expect her to graduate from high school. What do you think?"

As we chatted, I noticed that several other mothers, kids in tow, were waiting to talk with me. I wanted to give her as much time as she needed but not make the others wait. Luckily she saw them, too.

"I better not keep you; everyone needs a chance," she said. I gave her a hug and told her that I hoped her granddaughter would be chosen in the lottery.

No matter if we met them at a bus stop or in a church basement, almost every single parent filled out the one-page form and entered our lottery. We quickly had more applications than available spots. After we filled a short waiting list, I asked Yohana and Diallo to stop recruiting. I did not want a long waiting list: I thought it would be unnecessarily harsh for hundreds of parents to experience the heart-break of losing.

The very first lottery of Harlem Village Academies—which would later be called HVA for short—took place on April 1, 2003. Seventy-four students were offered admission. The parents knew that their children had just won a golden ticket, that without this school their child would be trapped, indefinitely, in a failing public school.

"This school is a blessing!" exclaimed Jasmine's grandmother when she found out they'd won the lottery. We hadn't even opened our doors yet.

Throughout the spring, Yohana called all the families whose names had been pulled in the lottery. Many she reached right away; others were less responsive and she had to call five or six times. She was fluent in Spanish, which was helpful since some parents did not speak English, and my Spanish was limited to counting to ten. Eventually she reached everyone, arranged their registration and uniforms, and gave them the date for our orientation.

During orientation, Yohana spent most of the day in the auditorium going over the school calendar and answering parents' questions while I supervised the student diagnostic testing. My three kids acted as gofers between us.

When most of the students had settled into their testing and I was no longer needed in the classrooms, I went into the auditorium to chat with parents. Victoria's mother, Nicole, and father, Lemar, were sitting together reading through our family handbook. Nicole spotted me and asked to talk about Victoria. "She's shy and sweet, but she's teased all the time. She doesn't have many friends," Nicole said. They had been told that Victoria had a minor learning disability. She had been getting C's and D's, and she just didn't care anymore. "What really upsets me," Nicole said, "is that I don't think she has any dreams."

In May, we moved into our temporary building at 120th Street and started getting ready for Kareem, Brandon, Jasmine, Victoria, and the rest of our first fifth-grade class. I turned a hallway storage closet into my office and shared it with a part-time assistant and a few mice. We couldn't get up out of our chairs at the same time without crashing into each other.

By June, we had cleaned up the place, but we needed furniture. A group of us decided to make the trek to IKEA in New Jersey. During the startup years, I took my kids with me everywhere. Generally, they enjoyed helping out, but they weren't particularly excited about spending an entire Saturday shopping for chairs, desks, and bookshelves. Luckily, *Harry Potter and the Order of the Phoenix* had just come out, so while I searched for furniture, they happily spent the afternoon in the children's department reading on the beds, glued to J. K. Rowling and oblivious to the shoppers around them.

That summer, I thought about our school every second. At Starbucks, I noticed their small chalkboards with the daily coffee specials handwritten in colored chalk. It was a nice touch that gave customers a warm and welcoming feeling. That inspired me to buy a few little chalkboards to place at our entrance with welcome messages, a word of the day, and quote of the week. Another idea came to me in a cute shop that we'd stopped into in Chappaqua. I had spotted some beautiful pencil drawings of distinguished authors and poets. They were two hundred dollars each but the shop owner gave me the phone number of the local artist, who was kind enough to make us complimentary photocopies. We placed them in $1.99 Wal-Mart frames and hung them in our hallways. At Barnes & Noble, I noticed a new wrapping paper featuring colorful sketches of vintage books that would be perfect for our bulletin boards. The manager donated some. All these small details, I hoped, would create a warm and inspiring academic environment.

We had to save our Gates Foundation grant for salaries during our first few years because there would be a huge gap between our state revenue and the actual cost of running a new school. We would have to be creative. I asked everyone I knew to donate what they could. My neighbors organized a book drive through the Westchester Girl Scouts. I would often step outside my front door to find a box of books that someone had dropped off the night before. Friends donated conference tables and file cabinets, and my mom provided posters and plants to spruce up the offices. I brought in my collection of CDs so our students would be exposed to Tchaikovsky, Beethoven, and other classical composers during arrival, dismissal and transitions—so much better than those jarring school bells.

Finally, the Saturday before we were set to open, my three kids and I got to work at the school. I placed a bouquet of flowers on each teacher's desk to express how much I appreciated their dedication. Avi put together bookshelves, while Chava organized and labeled library books and Rachel started on posters. Over the years Rachel would spend hours designing and perfecting the HVA posters. She was also the official HVA teachers' birthday cake baker.

At 4 p.m., as teachers were putting final touches on their classrooms and lesson plans, the janitor gave us a heads-up that the building would be closing in an hour. It would not reopen until our first day of school. As soon as he said that, my heart started racing and I started feeling butterflies as I thought about Kareem, Brandon, Jasmine, and Victoria. In just a few days, these children would be entrusted to our care.

I took a deep breath, grabbed a notebook, and walked into an empty corner classroom. Sitting at a student desk in the back, I started writing. I poured my dreams for our children—the ideals I hoped they would embrace—onto the paper.

In college I had studied the meaning of prayer—saying words out loud to set the right intention for each day—and the connection between thought, speech, and action. I wanted our students to recite something on the first day of school—words that would set the tone for our community.

"Education is my birthright" I wrote for Kareem. And as I wrote about "personal dreams," I thought of Victoria—and I thought of Christopher again.

Education is my birthright
Education is the birthright of all children
Education is the path to freedom
The freedom to achieve my personal dreams
Education is the path to justice
Justice for every man, woman, and child
Education is the path to power
The power to change the world
Education is the path to joy
The joy of learning is a privilege
Education is my full-time job
Education requires hard work
I recommit myself this day
I recommit myself to focus on my studies
I recommit myself this day

I recommit myself to honor my teachers
I recommit myself to respect
To respect for myself and my fellow students
I recommit myself to scholarship
To training my mind and pushing myself to work hard
I recommit myself to kindness
To going out of my way to be kind to others
I recommit myself to our community
I recommit myself to our community

CHAPTER 10

DROWNING

IT'S GOING TO BE PERFECT. When the alarm rang at 4:45 a.m. on September 9, 2003, that was the first thought that drifted through my groggy mind.

I had done everything to prepare. I had called the Riviera Bake House, the best bakery in Dobbs Ferry. At 6 a.m. I'd zip in and pick up chocolate croissants—a first-day treat for my teachers. I had arranged for a neighbor to be available in case of emergency. The kids, now in seventh, eighth, and ninth grade, and I had discussed their plan for getting ready without me that morning. I had filled my father's old blue car with gas the night before. I had even set out my clothes: plain black slacks from the Gap, a blue sweater, and black flats—practical and easy to throw on without thinking.

It felt as if I had been waiting my whole life for this day. And for the past two years, I'd been working toward it. I put the kids' lunch bags on the kitchen table, and I cut up an apple for myself and put it in a sandwich bag. An apple on the first day of school—perfect.

The students would be on time and looking sharp in their new uniforms: khaki pants, light blue oxford shirts, and navy blue sweaters. I would be positioned at the top of the stairs at our building at 120th Street fifteen minutes in advance, standing with my clipboard and a loving smile, ready to welcome them one by one. "So happy you are here," I would say to each child individually. I would ask all the boys and girls to tell me one thing about themselves so that I could try to get to know the students that very first morning.

It did not turn out the way I had imagined. Not even close.

When I got to our school, it was pouring rain. The building was locked and completely dark, and there wasn't a security guard or custodian in sight. Unhappy students were standing outside in the rain, their new uniforms quickly becoming damp. My teachers, who arrived an hour early so that they could prepare, instead spent that hour standing outside the building. Now, despite being drenched, they tried to keep the students in good spirits, though at least two of the kids were already on the verge of tears.

I was beside myself. Why hadn't I thought to remind the building management on Saturday that they had agreed to open the doors early? Why hadn't it occurred to me to ask for the cell phone numbers of our janitors, Angel and Andy, just in case? Why hadn't I realized that we should ask the building manager to give us our own backup key?

It was the first five minutes of our first day, and already I'd made a mistake that negatively impacted our entire community of teachers and students. It was the first of about a thousand I would make during the next eight years.

When the doors finally opened at 8:15, it was a mad rush to get the entire student body into the building. Diallo, our operations director who soon became the dean, directed students to proceed to their homerooms. Each classroom had been named after a college, one of several ideas I had learned from the successful KIPP schools.

All morning Yohana fielded questions from parents about missing forms, MetroCards, school supplies, and uniforms. She answered all queries patiently, with a soothing tone and a laugh that made everyone adore her. Meanwhile, Diallo dealt with the children whose uniforms were soaked (he had lots of spares) or incomplete. The teachers helped their new students dry off and introduced them to one another.

At 8:45, Diallo pushed "play" on our jerry-rigged speaker system. The sound of Vivaldi's *Four Seasons* signaled it was time for our first all-school morning meeting. At home, I played classical music, and I was looking forward to doing the same with my students. Each week they would listen to a different composer from my CD collection. Though I hadn't said so explicitly, I hoped this would counteract the effects of popular music videos, whose harsh, violent lyrics coarsen children's susceptible minds. School would be a calm sanctuary, a place where our students would be protected from the city, a place of soul and warmth where they could learn and be happy.

Each class filed into the auditorium and the teachers directed kids to sit in rows on the stage. As the music played and the students took their seats, I felt humbled and overjoyed. These fifth graders had been attending district public schools in Harlem, East Harlem, and the South Bronx where they statistically had only an 8 percent chance of making it to college. Now they were *our* children.

I had prepared a short morning message for each of the first three days of school. Today's theme would be "We're strict because we love you." Tomorrow would be "I am the leader of my life"—an idea about student leadership that had been inspired by Mel during my summers at camp. The talk on day three would focus on self-discipline.

I looked at the boys and girls sitting in front of me. For a moment, I had a flashback to summer camp, when I was seventeen and speaking in an old white building in front of some four hundred kids, also sitting on the floor in complete silence, as I talked about the importance of social activism.

But this was not summer camp and I was not their peer. The stakes for our students couldn't be higher. A good education would be life-changing. I had to make it immediately clear that in our school, the adults are in charge. That sense of authority, I knew, would allow our students to feel safe, cared for, and ultimately, happy.

"We are so pleased to welcome you here," I said, smiling broadly and making eye contact with every single child. "But I need to tell you something right from the start." Then I paused, stopped smiling quite so brightly, and crossed my arms.

"This school is *completely* different." I paused again, a technique that I had learned from Mel, and then repeated, like he always did when he wanted to get our attention. "This school is *completely* different from any school you've ever been to. Here's why. We are very, very"—I looked around and repeated myself for emphasis—"*very* strict."

My comportment, expression, and tone all sent one message: I am in charge. Misbehave at your own risk.

"Now, who can raise a hand to tell me: why do you think we're so strict?" I asked, raising my own hand to emphasize the instruction.

Only two students dared to raise their hands.

"So we'll follow the rules?" a sweet girl with curly short hair offered.

"Thank you. You may put your hand down." I said, exaggerating the tenor of strictness for effect on this first day.

"So we'll stay out of trouble?" suggested a little boy

I looked at as many of them individually as I could. "Any other suggestions?" I asked, with a deliberately firm tone.

Silence.

"We're strict"—I paused yet again to give maximum impact to what I was about to say—"because we love you." And the students saw me smiling, beaming, actually. I looked at them, each precious face, so hopeful. I don't know how it happened so fast, but I just fell in love with the kids sitting in front of me.

"We love you," I repeated. "We're strict because we love you."

Years later, when they were in high school, a few of these fifth graders would tell me that day was the first time they had heard a principal or a teacher use the word *love* in school.

"We're strict because we care about you. Think about it: If we didn't love you then we'd let you just do whatever you want. 'Who cares?' would be our attitude. But we do care."

I stopped smiling and shifted back to my authoritative expression. "We know what's best for you," I said. "And we have *lots* of rules." Then I lowered my voice and leaned in to the group. "Here's how it works at this school: Every student follows every rule," I said softly. "No ifs, ands, or buts. That's the way it is here. No exceptions." I repeated, this time very slowly, emphasizing each word, almost in a whisper: "Every. Student. Follows. Every. Rule." Then, enthusiastically, channeling Mel: "We are a community. We are a family."

The teachers saw me signal to them, and they started handing out copies of the student pledge. I told the students that we would say the pledge each morning. In future morning meetings, I explained, the students in the "advisory of the week" would select the music of the week, select the word of the day, and lead the pledge. But on this first morning I would lead it. "This is our school's pledge. I will call out the first line and you will respond with the next line."

"Education is my birthright. Now you say—"

And the students responded: "Education is the birthright of all children."

"Education is the path to freedom—"

"The freedom to achieve my personal dreams."

I continued, "Education is the path to justice—"

It was powerful watching these nine- and ten-year-old boys and girls recite these words—words that were, for me, the most personal prayer I had for them. I just hoped I would be able to lead the school effectively to help them fulfill their God-given potential.

My plan after the morning meeting was to head directly to the classrooms so I could support teachers, run interference, and help solve problems. But before I could make it to the first classroom, I heard yelling in the hallway. A father and daughter stood with Diallo. "A minute late isn't late!" the dad shouted. He was enraged that Destiny, his daughter, hadn't been permitted to enter morning meeting. We had explained the importance of timely arrival to all of our parents at family orientation in June, and Diallo was standing by the rules. Now the father wanted to speak with me.

Listening to his frustration, I was genuinely sympathetic and I told him as much. "I'm a parent also. I get it. I know how hard it is to get kids out the door in the morning." Then I explained the reasons why we could not make exceptions—that our school had high standards, that ultimately these rules were best for students, since being on time would help them learn to be responsible. Most important, I tried to explain that missing some crucial information during the first few minutes of a lesson could make it very hard for that student to follow along for the entire class period.

He wasn't having it. "Give me a break. A minute late isn't late!" he repeated. Other parents were standing in the hallway watching our interaction, and Destiny had been next to her father the whole time. I suddenly realized my mistake: I should have gotten Destiny into first period before anything else. I suggested that perhaps we should get his daughter to class and the two of us could continue the discussion in private another time.

"Come with me, honey," I said to Destiny as I walked her to the classroom. Yohana caught up with us and whispered to me that Ms. Jones, another parent, was sitting in my office waiting to speak with me. "Could you ask her to wait a little, or see what she needs?" I asked

Yohana. Before I left the classroom, I quickly scribbled, "Next Year" on top of the second page of my notebook and wrote, "Figure out advance instruction on timely arrival!"

As I walked down the hall toward my office to speak with Ms. Jones, another parent, Mrs. Franklin, stopped me. "Dr. Kenny, do you have a second?" She wanted to let me know that she was displeased that we had no gym and no sports program. "The children really need that." I assured her that we would work on it.

Worried that I had kept Ms. Jones waiting, I started speed-walking down the hall to my office. "Do you have a second?" Yohana said as I walked through the door. "Staples won't deliver the supplies we wanted by tomorrow because we don't have an account. Oh, and the lunch is going to be late because they got our school number wrong. Should I tell the teachers that we need to adjust the schedule? Or will you do that?" I scribbled down everything she said on the top page of my notebook, which I had designated "today," with a huge circle around "teacher schedule/late lunch." I had to think quickly. "Okay, you be resourceful and figure out the supply issue, and I'll figure out the schedule just as soon as I meet with this parent."

I apologized to Ms. Jones for making her wait so long. "I'm not sure if you remember me. I'm Joseph's mom," she said.

"Sure I remember, nice to see you. Is everything okay?" I asked.

"Well, not really," she said. "It's Joseph. He can't . . . he has a . . . he's—" Before she could get the words out, she started crying. "I'm sorry," she said. "I've just been so frustrated with the schools."

"It's fine," I said, handing her a tissue. "Whatever it is, we want to help."

She explained that Joseph did not know how to read, and yet he had been promoted every year since kindergarten. "I don't know what's wrong. I don't know why my baby can't read, and every year they push him on because he doesn't make trouble," she sobbed.

"We're going to figure this out," I promised. "I'd like to speak with Joseph after school for a bit. Is that okay?" I gave Ms. Jones my cell number. "I'll call you by the end of the week, but you can call me any time," I offered. Quickly I started another notebook page called "students" and wrote down Joseph's name with a few notes.

As I walked Ms. Jones to the door, I saw a mouse scamper behind the file cabinet. I almost squealed but caught myself. "Deal with mice!" got its own dedicated page in my notebook.

My meeting with Joseph at the end of that first day would be the beginning of a multiyear journey. I wrote down three words in front of him—*go*, *cat*, and *bring*—and I asked Joseph what he saw. "The letters are dancing on the page," he said. "The words are jumping around." It would take many months of hard work from his teachers and our special education consultant to begin to help Joseph. By February, he had made some progress, but not nearly enough. So I sent my kids to spend their winter vacation week with their grandparents while I pored over research studies in the field of reading remediation. I came upon two programs that looked promising, and we found a trained tutor to come in four hours per week for Joseph. By the end of the year, Joseph was finally making progress. Within three years he was reading close to grade level and by tenth grade he was reading *Romeo and Juliet*, and had passed all the required Regents exams.

It was 10:30 a.m., I'd been up since 4:45, and I realized that I still hadn't eaten my apple. I had forgotten to eat anything. Just when I was about to take it out of my bag, the school phone rang. Yohana was off solving the lunch crisis and nobody was in the office so I went over to the phone and picked it up. "This is Dr. Kenny. How may I help you?" As I started talking with the parent on the line, I glanced down and saw a large stack of messages on my desk that had accumulated in the last few hours.

No sooner had I hung up the phone than the music started playing—it was time for another hallway transition. Monitoring the halls during transitions between classes was one of the many practices I had learned from the other charter schools, and it made so much sense. Adult supervision was the most effective way to prevent the fighting that so often broke out in typical city middle schools. It also set a rhythm to the day and gave us a feeling of community.

But on day one, transitions were a disaster. Kids collided into each other, books thudded to the ground, and sometimes entire classes walked in the wrong direction. Why hadn't I realized that we'd need a more organized system?

Before I could finish writing "transition system" on my workout list, I heard a ruckus coming from the dean's office. It was only 10:45 and already six students had been sent out of class for misbehavior. In the dean's office, two girls sat brooding. Apparently both of them had reputations as bullies and were already acting rude in class.

As I looked around the dean's office, I recognized one of the boys right away. It was Sean, an incredibly cute nine-year-old I had hoped would make it into the lottery. What on earth could have landed him here on day one? "Why were you sent out of class?" I asked Sean. "I dunno," he mumbled without looking at me. This was not the tone of the sweet child I had chatted with at our orientation last spring.

"First of all," I said firmly but quietly, "you will speak in a respectful tone and you will look at me while I'm speaking." He glared at me. "Not like that," I said. I maintained my gaze, while making myself a mental note to talk about Sean later with his teachers.

Sean softened his expression. "Thank you," I said, reminding Sean that I knew he was better than his actions (an assumption I shared with every student, even the bullies). I spent another forty minutes in the dean's office talking with students, figuring out what was going on, and jotting down notes.

No matter the situation, my expectations, my tone, my words—my entire approach—was to treat every child as if he or she were my own. I realized that there were vast worlds of psychological and pedagogical information that I lacked. But I did the best with what I had, which was the sincerity of my love and respect for them.

Vivaldi interrupted my thoughts—time for (late) lunch.

During lunch I went into Nick's classroom to look for Destiny. She had just finished eating and I wanted to grab a few minutes with her. "Come with me, honey; let's sit on the bench together and talk about what happened this morning." I told Destiny that starting tomorrow I expected her to get herself to school on time, and we explored the many reasons why being on time would be important to her future success. "If you're competing for a job with three other people and they show up early but you're late, what kind of impression do you think that will make on the boss?" I asked. "And if you were the boss, what would you think of someone giving you an excuse?"

Then I asked her lots of questions about whether she had her own alarm clock, which train she took, how long the commute was from her house to school, and more. I asked her to take out a notebook. "We're going to work backwards from when you have to be at school so that we can make sure you're on time every day, okay? Let's call it your 'timely arrival plan.'" She started writing.

"So if the cutoff for arriving on time for school is 7:40 a.m.," I said, "you will plan on being here at 7:25. Why do you think you should plan for 7:25?" I continued with a series of questions, tips, and organizational time-savers like setting out her clothes and packing up her backpack the night before. I asked what problems she had usually encountered in the past in trying to get to school on time, and we brainstormed solutions one by one.

As a mother, I had one more concern. I wanted to make sure she would get at least eight hours of sleep, nine if possible. So we went backward further still, figuring out together what time she would need to go to sleep in order to get at least eight hours. Finally, I said,

"Let's add a half an hour so that you can get into bed with a book and read before lights out!" I didn't know if this was realistic, since I didn't yet have a good sense of Destiny's home life, but it was worth a try.

Finally, I addressed the issue of the rain as an excuse for being late. "What do you think happens in New York City on a rainy or snowy day? Do you think the trains and buses are faster or slower?" She got my point: leave even earlier. No excuses, and find a solution to every problem, regardless of the circumstances

I brought Destiny back to her class to join the other kids who were chatting as they tossed empty milk cartons into the trash. With no cafeteria, lunch was held in classrooms. One of the problems I noticed, however, was that the garbage bins were too small. By the end of lunch, they overflowed, signaling the potential for a major cockroach situation. I was about to write "garbage bins" on the same page as "mice" when Diallo saw me and mentioned that he had already planned to pick some up. "You are the best, thank you!" I said, crossing it off my list.

It was time for recess, but the rain hadn't let up, so we had to hold it inside the auditorium. It was far from ideal, but we let the kids run around, and everyone pitched in to make it as fun as possible. I noticed a student, Jamar, pretending his hands were a gun and making shooting sounds at the other kids. I walked over to Jamar and let him know that he was not allowed to pretend to shoot anyone. "It's not a big deal," he told me. "Yes, it is," I said.

As we got to talking, Jamar mentioned casually that there had been a shooting in his local movie theater on Sunday night. (When I looked into it later on, I discovered that Jamar was right.) "Were you there, or did you hear about it from someone else?" I asked. He was there. "Was anyone hurt?" He acted unfazed. "Nope, nobody was killed, it was just a shoot-out." *Just* a shoot-out?

A ball came bouncing across the room and nearly hit my head. Jamar caught it and laughed. "Can I go?" he asked.

"Yes, have fun," I said, "but no more fake shooting, you got—?"

Before I could finish my sentence, I heard a screech and a lot of laughter. Stephan, another ten-year-old boy, had been running on the other side of the auditorium and now he'd slipped and fallen. The laughter stopped very quickly as his classmates realized he was in real pain. Diallo was on top of the situation, which turned out to be a sprained ankle. Our school facility was deficient in that it didn't include a gym, but my plan—making the best of what we had by holding recess in the auditorium—was another one of my many mistakes that day.

It was 1 p.m. and I was finally ready to get into classrooms to observe teachers.

"Hey, I have this block off. I'm going out to grab coffee; do you want anything?" Nick asked.

"Oh my God, thanks, I'd love a peppermint tea." Just then I realized I was hungry and my apple had gotten brown sitting in the sandwich bag for seven hours. Luckily Rebecca had brought in pretzels, and she encouraged me to take some. But I really wanted to pop my head into each classroom during the first twenty minutes of the block to see how each teacher began their lesson.

Just before we split up—Nick to coffee, me to class—we heard a teacher yelling at students. Not reprimanding firmly, not correcting, but yelling. I hesitated for a moment and we looked at each other. I didn't say anything. After Nick walked down the steps, I jotted a quick note on my workout page to remind everyone that we do not yell at students. I spent the afternoon in and out of classrooms, writing down all the great things I saw to share later with the team, as well as the areas that needed improvement.

When Vivaldi came on for the last time that day, and we got the children out the door, my teachers looked ready to pass out. But all we could talk about was the kids—the things they did that were cute, the things they said that were funny, the things that went wrong.

As we sat around the conference table together eating and laughing, I was reminded of our very first workout that summer. I had asked the teachers to spend ten minutes filling out a worksheet at the beginning of the session. The worksheet made no sense and had nothing to do with the topics we discussed. Then at the very end of the meeting, I asked for feedback. Nobody had anything candid to share. "What about the opening activity, the worksheet?" I had asked. They looked at each other and I started smiling. Nick got it. "That was a joke?" he asked. "Yes!" I replied. "Why didn't you guys say anything?" I asked. Rebecca later told me they had been nervous about speaking out. That was precisely why I had done it. I wanted to break down the formal hierarchy that they had been so used to in their previous schools. "We're colleagues," I said. "I'm completely open to your feedback. We're all in this together." That sense of equity and candor became a hallmark of our organization as we grew.

Here we were again at a workout, the concept we had adapted from GE's Jack Welch, and now we were tackling real issues. I kicked things off by sharing the great things I saw that day. Then I reminded everyone that workouts were dedicated to constructively solving problems together and that I would not burden them with administrative announcements.

In this workout, and in many subsequent ones during our early years, every problem that we solved became a new system or a new tradition that was created by teachers. Most of them took hours and hours to create, then many more hours year after year to refine. When students were unorganized, we created a homework folder system. When students didn't hand back signed forms, we created parent receipt and sticker systems. When students came to school tired and unprepared, we created the "HOURS" tradition, to teach them how to spend their evening hours at home constructively: the H was for Homework, O for Organize, U for Unwind, R for Read, S for Sleep (nine hours). For the rest of the year, I would stand at the top of the stairs and whisper to departing kids, "In bed with a book by eight, asleep by nine!" Between the startup year and our first two years of running that first school, we had solved hundreds of problems, and created dozens of small and large systems and traditions.

As we talked about all of the issues that had come up on that first day alone, Yohana walked into the room. "Oh my God," she said, laughing. "Dismissal took forty-five minutes! I had planned for it to take five." Here was yet another system in need of improvement. We would eventually hold hundreds of workouts every week over several years. But on that first day, what we all felt was our idealistic vision colliding with reality.

I got into my car at 7:25 p.m., threw my bag and notebook on the passenger seat, and looked at the housing project just to the left and the school building in front of me. Instead of putting the key in the ignition, I sat there in the parking lot, frozen. I glanced at my notebook, at the vast list of concerns and tasks that I'd accumulated in just one day.

I had filled seven pages of my notebook, top to bottom, with tasks. I would stay up until 1:30 that first night going through my notes, following up on everything I could, and getting organized for the next day. In my mind everything was urgent. It was simply a matter of what degree of urgency: Which tasks must be done tonight? Which can wait until tomorrow? What can wait until next week?

I'd committed my life to this work, and I was not questioning that commitment. But on that first day, I was drowning. Years later I would realize that I felt overwhelmed because each day I wanted to eradicate the educational inequity in Harlem *that day*.

"Helloooooo!!! I have to close the gate!" the night janitor called out.

"Sorry, Andy! Good night. Thank you!"

CHAPTER 11

MY CHILD IS
A CHILD AGAIN

DAY TWO, 6:30 A.M. I AM on the Saw Mill River Parkway, thinking about Damon, a cute, mischievous ten-year-old boy who had been sent out of class twice the previous day for disruptive behavior. While sitting in the dean's office, he had told me that he wasn't doing anything wrong. Last year in fourth grade, he said, "I was cursing and getting into fights all the time. They didn't make us go to the dean like at this school. The kids ran around; we didn't learn, 'cause the teacher just yelled at us. Kids were mean. Kids fight and hurt you. But it's no big deal."

No big deal. It was no big deal, he thought, that fourth-grade children did not feel safe at school, did not feel obligated to act nicely to one another. Of course it wasn't his fault. He was just a little boy. He didn't know that it did not have to be this way.

I was no longer reading about failing schools in Jonathan Kozol's books. Now I was seeing the impact of these schools as I spoke directly with the children who had suffered in them.

Damon was quite the talker, so it wasn't hard to get him to tell me more. "I played around in the halls with the rest of the kids. One day, we threw empty soda cans into classrooms and ran away. It was fun. We threw pencils out of the window to see if we could drop them onto the teacher cars in the parking lot. The teachers found out and they said I was a bad kid, and I'm stupid."

I asked how he felt about that. "I don't care," he said.

"Really?" I replied. "I don't believe you." Suddenly his carefree demeanor changed to a mixture of sadness and anger.

"You don't know me," he said.

"You're right," I replied. "But I do know that you're smart. I know that you would rather feel safe than to be in fights every day. I know that you are a leader. You're going to do great things with your life."

He let his guard down ever so slightly and smiled at me. "I am a leader, that's true," Damon said. "When I go running down the halls, and stuff, other kids do follow me."

"Well, I can tell you right now," I said, "you're not going to be behaving that way here. I won't allow it. I expect more from you."

"I don't like the rules," he said. "I don't like it. I don't like the uniform. I don't like the morning meeting." He was clearly testing whether I was serious and whether I cared. I knew he had hardships at home but I wasn't about to let that become an excuse. What he needed was for me to believe in his ability to overcome those obstacles.

"That's okay, you don't have to like it," I replied. "But you'll still do what I say. We all talk and act nicely to each other. That's how it is at this school. You will respect your teachers. You'll be nice to the other kids. That's just the way it is here."

"Whatever," he said, looking away.

"No, not whatever," I replied with a quiet but firm tone. "Look at me, please," I said. He looked at me but with a scowl. "Without the attitude," I insisted. He complied. "You will not use the word *whatever* with me. It's not respectful. And I won't use it with you. Are we clear?"

"Yes," he said.

In the same way that their former schools had failed to teach basic reading and math skills, they'd also failed to teach kids the basics of respectful and scholarly behavior—like being nice, paying attention, or waiting one's turn to speak. For most students, their default mode was to slouch, space out, mumble, fidget, or disrupt class. These habits made it incredibly difficult for teachers to maintain control of the class, let alone teach a lesson.

Lack of respect was something students like Damon had learned. As far as I was concerned, he could unlearn it. It might take a month, or a year, or two years, but we would see to it. Cursing, fighting, and flagrantly ignoring teachers' instructions at such a tender age isn't natural behavior for children. Damon would become a much happier kid if he behaved well in school. For God's sake, I thought, he's only ten years old.

The kind of chaos our students had experienced in their previous schools had created two problems. First, it had forced them to grow up too soon, to give up the carefree joy that is childhood. As I looked at their gestures and comportment, I could see they had learned to develop a harsh exterior to survive the mean city streets and hallways of city schools. Second, the lack of structure in their former schools led to a lack of learning, which led to low self-esteem, which in turn made them care less about learning.

The teachers and I needed to create a respectful and orderly environment so they could teach.

In order to get students to behave, all of the best urban schools I had visited had created elaborate systems of reward and punishment. The rewards ranged from "scholar dollars" that could be redeemed for prizes at the end of the week to points on a chart to weekly auctions. The punishments ranged from demerits and detention, to losing privileges or being placed on in-school suspension. I felt strongly that incentives and consequences were not the best way to influence behavior. I believed schools should *teach* children to behave with "preventive discipline" strategies: clarifying expectations, establishing routines and practicing them, speaking with a tone of authority, and building relationships with students. And the most important preventive discipline strategy of all was an interesting, challenging, and well-planned lesson. I felt so strongly about all this that I took a huge risk: we were the only charter school we knew of that opened our doors without a reward and demerit system for behavior.

We were trying to create a school for our children, and this was the vision our teachers had signed up for. I would never have dreamed of using incentives to get my own children to behave. I would never have said, "Be polite to the babysitter and I'll give you candy" or "Do your homework and I'll give you a dollar." I wanted my own children to learn good character for its own sake: to do the right thing because it's the right thing to do. Our Harlem children deserved the same.

As I observed each classroom on that second day, I could see that the students felt every teacher's love and dedication. But I noticed right away that the same students behaved completely differently depending on the teacher. The same students would behave perfectly in one room, average in another, and poorly in a third. The number of students sent out of class to the dean's office grew as each hour passed. I asked myself, How can we get students to behave well in *all* classes, all the time?

By mid-morning, I arrived at the last classroom at the end of the hall. I had expected to spend about twenty minutes in Rebecca's room, just as I had done in the others. But as I watched her teach, I could not get up from my chair. Rebecca was completely in her element in front of the classroom, like a virtuoso musician in the middle of playing, completely in the zone. The academic instruction was impressive. But what fascinated me was the subtext that flowed throughout her lesson. It was a subtext of constant, nonpunitive behavioral corrections.

Rebecca was soft-spoken but firm. "Brandon, sit up straight," she said, and when he responded by sitting up halfway she fixed her gaze on him and said "*really* straight."

Even as she spoke about academics, her eyes were on every student. She made sure that literally every single student was listening and looking at her, and speaking only when called on.

"Class, show me you're ready to learn. Sit up and look forward."

"Brandon, put your head up."

"There will be no kids who show up tired to this class."

"Jasmine, sit up so I know you're really listening."

Rebecca's corrections were made constantly, it seemed every minute, and they were targeted very specifically to particular students who were even slightly off task.

"Destiny, you're looking at me, not out the window."

"Kareem, I need you showing me your effort."

She was determined to break the habits that their former schools had allowed. She created routines for every learning activity. Each routine included specific details for where, how, and what should be done, then she had students practice them over and over. It reminded me of something Mel used to say: "Repetition is education."

Rebecca broke her instructions down into very small pieces, and set up the students for success by telling them precisely what she expected. "We're about to transition to filing our papers into our binders and here's how it will work . . ." Just then, a student in the back of room jumped ahead and opened her binder. Rebecca caught it: "Victoria, do not start yet. I'm not done giving you the directions."

As much as I was intrigued by the number of behavioral directives—

she corrected students dozens of times every hour—what was even more fascinating was that Rebecca's behavior training somehow did not feel like the focus of the class. It was in the background, a subtext to a sophisticated academic lesson. The subtext of behavior corrections was like the music in a good movie, which enhances the dialogue, but doesn't distract from it.

Before long, I found myself writing down what amounted to a transcript of the lesson's subtext so that I could analyze it that night.

One of the keys was that Rebecca did not give general corrections. She was very specific about each student's name and each expected behavior. "Kareem, sit up. Victoria, eyes on me. Damon, listen to Victoria. Stephan: I can *not* teach with you like that. You've *got* to have your eyes on me so I know you are listening." All morning it went on like this.

During a vocabulary lesson, she asked "What do you think, Jasmine?—All eyes on Jasmine!" with lightning speed. Jasmine hadn't been listening and gave a so-so answer. Rebecca had a look of genuine disappointment on her face. That signaled to Jasmine and all the students that if they did not want to disappoint this amazing teacher they'd better pay attention.

Before every instruction, Rebecca scanned the room to make sure she had 100 percent of their eyes—before saying to them, "Okay, now here's what we will be doing with the spelling book." I spent several hours in Rebecca's class that second day, and managed to squeeze in visits to all the classrooms at least once more.

The next day I went back to Rebecca's room, where I found her already refining her own practices. "Yesterday I noticed there was some pushing and shoving during our dismissal, so I've set up a new routine. We will have a boys line and girls line, and you'll see the blue tape I've put on the floor where the lines begin." Then she would go on to describe a clear system she had devised to address the problem.

She exuded a sense of urgency that the students picked up on.

"We have a lot to learn so we're not going to waste any time in this class—*ever*."

In the classrooms I had seen throughout the city, the standards for behavior were so low that students regularly talked amongst themselves while the teacher was speaking. But in Rebecca's room, if a student so much as whispered to a neighbor in the next seat, Rebecca would glare at the student with the most incredulous look on her face and say something like, "Brandon, I'm *right* in the middle of teaching."

We had the same mix of students as those traditional public schools: we had a few kids in each class who would behave beautifully no matter what was going on around them, the majority of kids who were very impressionable and could go any way depending on the skills of the teacher, and of course the class clowns and bullies who tried to disrupt classes. In our first year, one of the bullies was a girl named Kayla. I had noticed Kayla on the first day during morning meeting, and all the other teachers noticed her as well. She had that "don't mess with me" look on her face. We later learned that her mother was abusive to her and that she, along with a bunch of our other students, had been suspended multiple times in their former schools. They repeated their bullying behavior from the moment they stepped foot in our school.

Kayla would intentionally try to disrupt class, but it didn't faze Rebecca. She handled Kayla each day with a combination of warmth and strictness that Kayla had obviously never experienced before. Sometimes Rebecca would take her aside for a one-on-one talk. During class she'd put Kayla in her place while showing the rest of the class that the teacher—not a ten-year-old—was in charge of this classroom. It wasn't just "Kayla, sit up straight" but rather "Kayla, get yourself sitting up with the rest of the class," or "Kayla, don't make me have to repeat the directions just for you; follow along with the class." Rebecca was basically taking her down a notch.

If Kayla so much as rolled her eyes, Rebecca stopped mid-sentence and stared her down, saying, "Kayla, you are *not* the boss of this class."

Rebecca was so well prepared that she was able to focus her full attention on every student during class. She had her lesson plans for the week organized and completed by Sunday night (although she tweaked them every afternoon for the next day). She always reread the books she was about to teach, even if she had read them several times before. She would never dream of doing what she called "teacher business," like grading a quiz, during a lesson.

She made her expectations so clear that they were easy for students to follow. "There are a few kids who were whining in class this morning. So now everyone is going to listen very carefully to what I'm about to say: If you whine to me, I will *never* do for you what it is you are whining about, because it's not respectful. When you whine, my ears just shut off! When you speak to me in a respectful tone, I will *always* try to help you." I thought her approach was perfect for fifth graders—"my ears just shut off!"—and when she actually followed through and only helped the students who spoke respectfully, all the kids realized she meant what she said. Day by day, and week by week, Rebecca was teaching these boys and girls habits that would shape them for life. She was teaching them to become respectful, focused, responsible students. This was what I wanted for our entire school, and for that matter, all schools.

That's why it was so disappointing to watch what happened to Rebecca's students in other classrooms.

Nick stopped me in the hall after lunch on Wednesday in early October. "You've been observing classes since school started and all you've given me are positive comments," he said. "But you spent a year observing in the best charter schools. What I'd really like to hear is feedback."

Here was one of the most experienced, outstanding teachers I'd ever seen—and all he wanted was feedback? His instruction was sophisticated. He designed each lesson with painstaking care to elicit students' deep thinking. And his students were absolutely falling in love with math!

But I realized that I hadn't been in his classroom for more than ten minutes in the last three weeks. I had focused my time on other teachers, where my help was more urgently needed. So I made a point of observing a full lesson from start to finish that day.

As I sat in the back, I immediately noticed that his students' behavior had gotten worse since the last time I had observed. Back in the first week, about 95 percent of his students had been behaving great, but now about a month later it was more like 75 percent. When Nick gave an instruction, most but not all students would follow it. When he spoke, most but not all students would look at him and listen. All this meant a bunch of students were missing out on what he was teaching. A few students even disrupted the lesson, so he had to occasionally send them out of class to the dean. As the weeks went by, more of his class time was spent dealing with misbehavior.

I had no ideas for the best way to teach double-digit multiplication, but I did have experience with overall instructional quality and behavior. We met at the end of the day, as Nick had requested. I started by sharing all that was great about his lesson. "You engage the students with an interesting question. And you're insisting that students do the intellectual heavy lifting to construct their own understanding of concepts. It's fantastic."

I meant every word. But Nick wasn't interested in all that. "Yeah, yeah, thanks! But what do you see that I could improve?"

I shared with him what I had seen that day. "Juan, Brandon, and Victoria were looking out the window and not taking notes when you were at the board. Kareem was playing with his pencil and not working at all, which is why he wasn't following ten minutes into the lesson, and at the end, Kalil had his head on the desk and didn't copy down the homework assignment. Jasmine and Marie were talking with each other when you were answering Diamond's question, which is why Jasmine didn't know the answer." And on I went, sharing with him the specific behaviors that had negatively impacted student learning. Now Nick was interested.

I told him that I had read somewhere that it took about seven weeks to establish new habits, and I shared with him all the strategies I could think of—everything I had learned from visiting other charter schools, from my own experience, and of course from observing Rebecca.

"It's going to be exhausting, honestly. But if you follow through on one hundred percent of the students meeting your expectations one hundred percent of the time, then in seven weeks the kids will internalize all these new habits. It will become second nature for them, and your classroom will be transformed."

Nick was totally game. For the next few weeks, he asked me to observe and give feedback again and again so that he could improve each day. By the end of the seven weeks, students were behaving at the same extraordinary level as they were in Rebecca's room. Fewer of Nick's students had to be sent out of class for disruptive behavior, and more of them than ever before completed homework and achieved higher quiz grades. Nick was pleased. "It really worked out well. I barely deal with behavior issues anymore," he told me.

I was impressed with his humility and capacity for refining his practice. But Nick was already exceptional. Some other teachers were struggling with poor student behavior. How could I get our entire school to function at a higher level?

I had been a public school parent for ten years. I had experienced what it was like when a school principal didn't know you or even viewed parents as a nuisance. So I could see why some of our parents might see me this way, too. Many of them told me they were used to being treated disrespectfully in their previous schools. I wanted them to be treated with the respect they deserved.

Schools sometimes blame parents for not being involved, but I told our team we should do our part by making them feel welcome. I decided to set a different tone from the beginning. We started by organizing small potluck dinners for teachers, parents, and students.

At our first potluck, Yohana and I chatted with the parents as they arrived. I asked as many of them as possible what they felt was going well and what needed improvement. After only a half hour, I had six pages of notes, which I planned to follow up on as fast as I could. After everyone had enjoyed the meal, I asked all the parents to sit in the chairs that we had arranged in a large circle, and I asked the students to sit on the floor in the middle of it.

Everyone settled. "Could we all please stand and hold hands?" I asked. I stood up and held hands with the two parents to my left and right. This one act immediately transformed the feeling in the room from a typical public school gathering to an intimate community. Something about the act of holding hands reminded everyone of the deeper connection that we all had to each other. As we stood in a circle, the children all looked up at us. I thought about the fact that most of us in the room were single mothers trying to keep our children on a straight and narrow path in the big city. That's hard to do on your own. So I began speaking to our new fifth graders as a representative of the adult community surrounding them. "As you look around, I want you to remember this day," I said. "Eight years from now, when you go off to college, you will think back on this day as the beginning of an important journey. We are here to love you and support you. All of us are in this together—your own parent or guardian or grandma, your teachers and I, and the parents of your classmates—we are all one big family. Now you have a responsibility, too. We expect a lot from you. We expect you to behave and listen to your teachers. We expect you to do all your homework, all of it, every night. We expect you to take your class work seriously. We will not let you get away with second-rate work because you are capable of excellence. We will be here for you no matter what. We are all your mother. We are all your father."

I looked across the circle and I saw a grandmother tearing up a bit. She didn't want to break the circle by letting go of hands, so she tried to wipe her eyes with her shoulder.

The children were smiling up at us and they seemed to have a contented glow. We were a village, a community, and we would raise these children together.

At the end of the first school year, I was at home in our driveway getting ready to go to our HVA family picnic. A neighbor saw me and the three kids packing up the car. "What a bummer that you have to work on Saturday!" she said. "It's not work," I replied. "We're going to a picnic!" My kids and I had fun that day—they played wheelbarrow races and Frisbee with our schoolchildren, and I chatted with teachers and parents. It occurred to me that any school principal who didn't enjoy a picnic with parents and students was in the wrong profession.

Back in October, I had noticed Rebecca changing the configuration of her students' desks from straight rows to small clusters of four to five desks. "The kids are ready for cooperative learning now," she told me. I was excited to see what would happen next.

Rebecca had spent a significant amount of her class time on behavior in the first seven weeks of the year while other teachers had jumped right into instruction on day two. Now it was the exact reverse. Rebecca's students were incredibly well behaved so she was able to move into creative and higher level learning activities, while almost every other teacher had to spend a significant—and continually increasing—amount of time dealing with problematic behavior. In some rooms, the behavior was so-so and students weren't learning much. In others, the teachers were becoming frustrated from constantly reprimanding disruptive students.

Then, in early November, the unthinkable happened. Dave knocked into Taylor by accident, Taylor assumed it was on purpose and pushed back, and before you knew it, we had our first fight. I was heartsick.

The week before Thanksgiving, we got together for an extra-long workout to discuss behavior. "We really need a demerit system," one teacher immediately suggested. "I understand, Deborah, how strongly you feel that punishment is not the answer, but we need something." I felt certain that preventive strategies like Rebecca's—teaching students to behave in the first place rather than reacting with punishments when they misbehaved—were the most effective. That was what I had always done in the classroom, as a mother, and even as a camp counselor. I knew that demerits would be used effectively and sparingly by teachers who were skilled at preventive discipline. But I feared that they would be used ineffectively and in place of preventive discipline by less experienced teachers, and that would result in a whole bunch of unhappy kids. But despite how strongly I felt about preventive discipline, I felt even stronger about listening to my teachers. They really wanted a demerit system.

So when the students returned from holiday break we introduced demerits at morning meeting. We prepared a document listing behavior expectations; on the bottom I added two lines that I hoped students would take to heart: "I am the leader of my life. I do the right thing because it's the right thing to do."

Through the winter and spring, the demerit system made a dent in student behavior. Things got a little better. But we continued struggling with discipline right up until June. In some classes, kids disrupted the learning, while in other classes it was so bad that the teacher had to send students out every day. Some students were so disrespectful that they made teachers cry. It wasn't the kids' fault. Their previous schools had not trained them properly. It was my responsibility as the school leader to figure it out.

In our second year, I was being pulled in too many directions. We had committed to opening our second middle school the following year, so we had to go back to the startup task list. I tried to focus on the educational quality at our first school, while at the same time recruiting a new team for our second school—not to mention overseeing facility development, community relations, operational issues, and fund-raising. There was so much to do every day, and time just sped by.

Time seemed to fly even quicker when it came to my own kids. I could hardly believe that my youngest, Rachel, was about to turn thirteen. It was already time to celebrate her Bat Mitzvah. We all still missed Joel, but we had gotten a little more used to living on our own.

When the big day arrived, Rachel sang the prayers beautifully and the congregation was moved by her sweet voice. She had inherited her love of music from Joel. And her speech was on the theme of love. "Before my father died, he said that if someone had to be sick, he was glad that it was him, instead of my mother," Rachel said. "However, my mother wished that it could have been her to be sick instead of him, so that he could have lived. They both cared more about the other than about themselves. My parents taught me by example the meaning of true love that I will always remember. My parents also taught me to care about other people, not to think what can I get out of life, but rather what will I give to the world."

Rachel took that lesson to heart. The next year, she organized a volunteer program by recruiting students from her school to tutor our fifth graders in Harlem on Saturdays. The program ran for four years. She had grown up to be a confident, independent thinker. But I still remember when she was little and ran out of the house without socks to play in the snow in her boots. "Rachel, put on socks. It's freezing. Everyone wears socks in the winter," I said. "Not in my world!" she replied blissfully.

The ceremony was wonderful and made it clear that our family was beginning to heal—so much so that my father decided it would be a perfect time to talk to me about dating again. "Why don't you try computer dating," he suggested when we were back at home after the party. I could not imagine putting my photo and personal information on the Internet, but I just thanked my dad and told him I wasn't interested. Later I learned that he took my girls aside and suggested they set up a profile on the "email machine" for me. "You can just see if anyone looks interesting for your mother," he suggested. "But grandpa," said Chava, by then in ninth grade, "what will I do if one of them asks me on a date?"

Student behavior in our second year had been better than in our first year, and dramatically better than the failing schools in the surrounding school district. But I was still holding onto our private school vision. Through that lens we were not even close to where I wanted us to be. We had too much variation in quality: engaging lessons that lacked rigor, or rigid instruction that lacked passion. And in too many classrooms there was a reactive, negative approach to discipline. I was still picturing the self-directed students at Sidwell, who behaved just fine.

So at the end of that second year, while our teachers were on summer vacation, I spent July reading, researching, and reflecting on my past mistakes. I decided that in our third year, I would take a different approach to discipline. Instead of imparting information by training teachers, I would facilitate teacher collaboration and tap into their collective talent.

Everyone returned from vacation for Summer Institute, our annual teacher development session that we held each August. We now had two schools: our new middle school, in its first year, and our original middle school, now in its third year. The faculty had grown so big that we filled an entire classroom.

I was committed to making our behavior A+ across the board, and suggested a new idea: a three-day student orientation filled with behavior lessons that the teachers could design. I shared a few pointers about how to create lessons on behavior, such as giving very explicit instructions about every detail of the desired behavior, taking a lot of time to practice the behaviors, making the lesson fun, respecting students' intelligence by discussing the rationale for rules, and engaging students by asking them to analyze models of exemplary and wrong behaviors. Then I reminded all the teachers that it's not just about stating an expectation, but also following through in September and October until the desired behaviors become second nature.

But those pointers were very brief. The real reason we were about to experience a breakthrough was that I was fully trusting the teachers and giving them complete ownership over the entire program.

"Think about your ideal classroom," I said. "How are students behaving, what is your dream?" I led the teachers through an exercise where they visualized their students behaving exactly as they wanted. "Now let's turn the vision into a plan by turning every one of your desired behaviors into a lesson," I said. They came up with all the ideas and plans from there.

"Since we're talking about our dream classroom," said a sixth-grade teacher, "I want the kids to really listen when I speak."

"That was in my visualization also," another teacher said. "To listen to me and to each other."

"But how do we turn that into a plan? I mean it's so hard to get them to listen sometimes. They start doodling or tapping their pencils."

"Well, at least they're not throwing their pencils," offered a new teacher.

"Right. That's because we sweat the small stuff," said a returning teacher. "It makes something like throwing a pencil inconceivable."

"How about spinning a pencil?" joked a third teacher.

"Are we going to allow sharpening pencils in the middle of a lesson? That drives me crazy. The kids come back to their desk after a minute of sharpening and I have to repeat what I said. So either the rest of the class gets bored or that one kid is lost for the rest of the lesson."

"What about the kid who keeps sharpening a pencil until you could use it to perform surgery?"

Everyone was laughing as they shared their pencil stories from hell.

"So what's our decision? We still need a plan."

"Let's say no getting up to sharpen pencils in the middle of a lesson. Period."

"Love it. And if they show up to class unprepared, that's a demerit. If we all agree, they'll so easily get used to it."

"Problem solved."

"Wait—hold on. I want to teach, not be giving out demerits all day to kids who need a pencil."

"Me, too."

"I think that's the whole point of preventive discipline. We need to think about preventing the problem in the first place, not punishing it after."

"Okay, so what if we get them in the habit of bringing six sharpened pencils to school each morning—it prevents them from missing part of the lesson to sharpen a pencil."

"Yes. Exactly. We teach them about organizing school supplies at night. Preparation: that should be the topic of our lesson."

"Let's do it."

Energized as they worked in teams, the teachers created more than a dozen lessons about behavior, some with skits and songs and posters and even practical jokes to make the lessons fun.

The collaboration process had been amazing, and everyone was now fired up to teach the lessons they had created with their colleagues.

During the first week of school, teachers supported and observed each other and shared feedback, which further strengthened behavior as teachers learned from each other. As a result, many, many more classrooms had that amazing feeling—a perfect balance of warmth and strictness.

Teachers picked up each other's ideas and the most effective practices became consistent school-wide practices—not because we imposed them, but because teachers recognized the value of consistency for middle school students. Mary, a brilliant writing teacher who joined us in the fourth year, invented a silent signal that students could use to show their agreement with what someone was saying. It was a great way to keep students engaged and active without disrupting the flow of the lesson. This signal—two fingers pointing back and forth from the forehead—became so popular that all our teachers now use it. This kind of thing repeated itself over and over. We spent dozens of workouts together discussing which rules and expectations would be consistent school-wide, which would be consistent within each grade level, and which would be individualized by teacher.

The pencil discussion had been one of many similar discussions that took place over the years that followed. We talked about organizing homework folders. Lunch behavior. Recess behavior. Arrival and dismissal. Entering and exiting the classroom. We talked about how to teach students to be honest, to be courteous, to disagree respectfully.

Our behavior lessons got better every year as our teachers kept improving them. In turn, our teachers got better at preventive discipline every year as they learned from the process of creating and teaching the behavior lessons, analyzing mistakes, and improving for next time.

One of those was Jason. When he started with HVA, he decided to teach a behavior lesson called "bring it back," which taught kids how to transition respectfully from fun to serious learning activities. "In my prior schools, my classroom management was good but not great," he said. "Sometimes I lost control because I struggled with how to get them back on task after fun and laughter. I usually ended up raising my voice, which defeated the whole purpose of making my lesson fun." He looked at prior HVA teachers' lesson plans and took the parts he liked, but left off the things he didn't like. Then he asked an experienced teacher for feedback and further refined his lesson plan. "The whole experience made me realize I had not been doing my best in my old school."

His higher potential was just beneath the surface. The next year he effortlessly commanded an entire auditorium packed with hundreds of students, firmly and lovingly. But if he'd been handed a prepackaged lesson that first year, Jason said, "I wouldn't have learned anything. What made me feel so motivated was the fact that it was mine."

Now when visitors observe our schools we get three reactions. First, they ask, "Do you pick your kids?" just like I had assumed when I had visited Rebecca's classroom eight years ago in Boston. It seems too good to be true. Second, they ask if they are in the "best" classroom, until they continue the tour and realize that in just about any classroom they go into, at any time of day in any one of our schools, students are behaving just as incredibly well. But above all, they ask,

"Do the kids always have so much fun while behaving this well?"

They have no idea what we've been through to get to this point.

Over the years we developed even more approaches to shaping student character. One group of teachers created "family meeting," where students meet with their advisors in small groups every Friday afternoon to talk about their problems. One day I walked into family meeting led by Nitin, a teacher we had recruited from the NYC Teaching Fellows. One boy had been teasing another boy in the class, and Nitin was facilitating an emotional dialogue between the two while all the other boys listened. The twelve-year-old boy who had done the teasing had just apologized. This in and of itself was incredible to me, considering the violent fights that happened daily in the schools where these boys had come from. But Nitin held the boy who had apologized to an even higher standard. Nitin looked right at him and said, "*Sorry* is just a word. What are you going to do differently next week?" This took my breath away. We hadn't handed down a scripted character education program. We trusted our teachers. And this kind of conversation was the result.

For many students, our nurturing and orderly school community is a lifeline. "At my old school, I was the target for bullying," one of our girls said. "I was angry and depressed. I thought about suicide a few times. Then one day a mean girl started talking about me, and I snapped. I punched her. That was the first time my parents found out that I was being picked on. Now I'm at HVA and no one teases me. If it wasn't for this school I don't know where my life would be."

Visitors often ask our students how our schools differ from their former schools. In one such discussion with seven students, I discovered something. "They give us a lot more homework and the kids are nicer here," offered one girl. "The classes are more interesting and the other kids are nice to me," a boy said. "The teachers don't let you get away with playing around, and everyone is nice." Every single child seemed to come back to that theme: the kids are nice. Then someone asked: "Why do you think the kids are nicer here?"

An eleven-year-old girl raised her hand. "Well, when we got here on the first day the principal and teachers talked with us about being kind to each other and said there is no teasing and no fighting at all. You have all the rules so nobody is going to hurt us. So we don't have to worry about being beat up or no bully will hurt us. That's why we don't have to act mean to each other, we don't have to show we are tough. So we can just be a nice kid."

At that moment, I fully understood what a mother had said to me years before: "Thank you for giving me my son back." I smiled at her but before I could respond, she hugged me and said, "My child is a child again."

CHAPTER 12

I USED TO THROW
MY BOOKS AWAY

EUGENE STARES AT HIS PENCIL. Sitting in the last row on the far left, he fidgets, looks out the window, and then plays with his pencil again.

All our new students are taking their first diagnostic reading test: an internal test that we designed to gauge their reading levels. As our teachers administer the test, I visit every classroom to see how things are going. A lot of the kids seem uncomfortable, and half of them have barely answered a few questions. Eugene hasn't written a single word on his paper. I step a little closer to his desk and see that he is on the verge of tears.

Eugene looks hard at his blank answer sheet, then looks up at me. I kneel down in the aisle next to his desk. "It's okay," I whisper. "We're going to help—I promise." With that he starts crying, even as he tries to hide his tears from his classmates. I offer to take him to my office, and he nods his head yes.

I get Eugene talking to me in my office by asking about his favorite sports teams. Once he relaxes, I ask about the test. His demeanor immediately changes: "It's a reading test," he shrugs. "I always fail reading tests."

Unfortunately, this fact hadn't seemed to matter much at his old school. There he'd been advanced from one grade level to the next—even though they had repeatedly failed to teach him to read.

As we discovered that year and every year after, most of our incoming fifth graders were reading somewhere between a kindergarten and third-grade level. Eugene's reading ability was equivalent to that of a kindergartner when he began at HVA. Five years of failure left him without the confidence necessary to even attempt to take the test that morning.

Every year we had students like Eugene—students whose prior schools had failed to teach them how to pronounce the sounds of vowels and consonants. We also had students who knew their letters but had not been taught how to pronounce words.

You can catch kids up in math, science, or social studies in two to three years. But not in reading. The underlying foundation of literacy begins from infancy with the development of neural pathways in children's brains. This kind of brain development can't easily be made up for with a few months, or even years, of good instruction.

And reading can't be broken down into discrete facts and skills. Reading instruction is complex and consists of many factors—phonics, fluency, vocabulary, comprehension—and it takes an enormous amount of personal attention to determine why a particular student is struggling.

Back in June 2002, I met Howard Fuller, the legendary founder of Black Alliance for Educational Options, at the first national charter school conference I ever attended. He opened his speech with the following: "February 1, 1960. Four students from A&T College in

Greensboro sat down at a lunch counter and demanded to be served. And here we are in 2002. Our students can sit down at a lunch counter. They will be welcomed. *But they can't read the menu.*"

Howard shared something even more chilling with me after the speech. People in the business of building prisons have a simple business model, he told me. They look at the fourth-grade reading failure rate in communities across the country, and they build jails in the communities where kids can't read. If children are illiterate by age nine, it's a safe bet that they will end up in prison as young men.

Watching Eugene struggle, I was reminded of Howard's cautionary words. I wondered what Eugene's life might look like five years from now if he continued to fail at reading. In front of me was a bright, innocent, beautiful child. Other schools had failed him. I refused to allow that to happen again.

For decades, Harlem had been one of the lowest-performing school districts in the nation, with shameful rates of illiteracy. In 2002, only 29 percent of fourth graders could pass a basic reading test. Even more disturbing was that each year children were in school the results were *worse*: By eighth grade, only 16 percent of Harlem students could read at grade level.

Some schools had to be doing it right, and I was determined to understand what worked in reading instruction.

My first step was to call the State Education Department. I asked for a list of all public schools in low-income neighborhoods where the majority of eighth graders passed the reading test. I didn't care if the schools were charter schools or traditional public schools, as long as they had no admissions requirements. I wanted to be sure that whatever I learned would be applicable to our students who were admitted by open public lottery. My plan was to take this list—I imagined there would be perhaps fifty schools statewide—and visit those with the best results.

When I didn't hear back from the education department, I called them again and they gave me the names and numbers of four schools. "Thanks so much," I said. "But would you be able to email the full list?" The person on the other line sounded confused. "That's it," she said.

"Um, okay—I wonder if there's a mistake. I didn't mean just Manhattan. We're interested in receiving the complete list for the state," I said. "That's *it*. I just gave you the list," she said. I couldn't believe there were only four public schools that met my criteria. But so be it; we'd visit all four.

Andrew, who had been instrumental in crafting our charter applications and eventually became an English teacher in our high school, came with me on the first of these school visits. We spent a whole day observing reading instruction and meeting with the school's best reading teachers. We talked with students during lunch and reviewed their binders, which were filled with materials including homework, quarterly exams, and weekly quizzes.

Almost immediately, I noticed something was amiss, but I didn't want to jump the gun, so I waited and kept observing. By the last class period, I couldn't shake it and I took Andrew aside to compare notes. "Did you see the daily practice worksheet?" I asked. "Yeah," he said, dismayed. "The curriculum is nothing more than test-prep." That's just what I had picked up on: the lead teacher had designed her unit plans, lesson plans, and quizzes all to align with the state-mandated test.

"Look at this." I said to Andrew. "This kid got a check-plus but two words were used incorrectly." I looked through paper after paper.

"Check out this one," Andrew whispered. "This kid got a five out of five, but the sentence doesn't make sense."

We later learned that the scoring rules of the state test give students a point if they make an attempt at using mature vocabulary in their essays *even if the words are used incorrectly.* I was disappointed to see that this school, considered one of the very best in the state, had designed their reading curriculum around the test. Their grading system aligned perfectly with the test's low standard: teachers explicitly taught students to "use big words," but the students were not corrected if the words were used imprecisely. This practice misled students into believing that they understood the meaning of certain words when they did not, that they knew how to write well when they did not.

It seemed that this school had reviewed old state tests, analyzed every question, understood exactly what was required for the right answer, and developed its entire reading and writing curriculum solely around the test. When I visited the other high-scoring schools, I found they had done the same thing.

This was nothing like the instruction I'd expect for my own children. I wanted them to study classic and contemporary great books in depth, analyze the text for meaning, and write coherent essays about complex themes. In their suburban school, that's just what they did.

If you measured success by test scores alone, these top few urban schools were "closing the achievement gap" with the best suburban schools. But not if you used my measure: what I wanted for my own children.

So each summer as we welcomed new teachers, I gave the same speech: "We are responsible for the test, but it does not define our curriculum. Aligning to the test is important but it's only a first step. It is critical that we enhance our course plans based on what we would want for our own children." The teachers, principals, and I were all passionately committed to our shared vision. That commitment would carry us through many difficult years as we tried to figure out how to teach at a high level while dealing with the enormous challenges of students whose prior schools had barely taught them how to read and write.

During the first two years, Rebecca and I constantly talked about reading and writing instruction. We wanted our schools to teach analytical reading of challenging texts at a high level. We wanted to inspire students to read for pleasure; improve their vocabulary; and catch them up to grade level. In addition, of course, we had to prepare them for the state tests by teaching fundamental skills. For the first two years, we tried to accomplish all this by doubling our English instruction time.

But by the middle of our third year, as Rebecca left to give birth to her first child, we were still struggling. I'd walk into one class and observe a teacher engaging students in challenging questions about a text that were strategically designed to improve their reading comprehension. Then I'd walk into another class and see students filling in simple answers to easy questions on a worksheet, which amounted to nothing but busywork.

Over the years I spent hundreds of hours learning as much as I could about literacy. I had tons of questions—and as soon as one was answered, I'd have more. How much time should be spent on skills? How do we prevent the summer backslide? Should we set up classroom libraries or a school library? What is the most effective approach to teaching vocabulary? How can we involve parents in our literacy efforts? How many levels should we expect our students to move up each year?

I had convened an optional Friday literacy meeting, open to all teachers, principals, and academic directors, in which we talked about everything from comprehension and vocabulary to writing and grammar. We read books and articles, hired experts, observed other schools, and shared ideas.

Emily was one of our regulars and she had a problem: Too many of her students were stuck on one reading level and she couldn't figure out why. The internal reading test we used was not giving her the information she needed. "At first I assumed there was nothing to be done," Emily said. "Both our schools had been using this test for years. And changing it would have required adjustments to the schedule." She thought it wouldn't happen. But in the end, that's precisely what we did: we gave the teachers freedom to change the internal testing and we adjusted the schedule to support the new plan. "It was a really big deal that teachers' ideas were taken so seriously," Emily said. Through the new reading test, she discovered an underlying problem that affected most of her eighth graders: their fluency was so far behind, it was slowing down their comprehension. Based on that data, she tweaked her lesson structure, and her students' reading levels started moving up.

The quality of instruction continued to improve overall slowly but steadily each year. I was not quite satisfied with the slow part: I was still hoping to see more dramatic improvement. So I set aside my books, notes, and lists and reconnected with our "school for my children" vision. I had wanted my own children to fall in love with reading. I felt this was so important that I had raised Avi, Chava, and Rachel without TV. Every few months they would complain about it, and my response was always the same: I distracted them by changing the subject. Amazingly, this worked for more than a decade.

Once they were in middle school, we changed from no TV to a weekly TV night, although I never gave in to cable. Instead, I filled every room in the house with books, crafts, and puzzles, and we went to the bookstore a lot. If they loved one kind of book, like a Harry Potter novel, I'd recommend something similar for them to pick up next, like *The Chronicles of Narnia*. I paid close attention to the things they liked and bought books to match their interests, such as the series of twenty-four illustrated books about animals that Rachel read over and over. All this effort brought out their natural love of reading from a young age and they ended up reading two or three books a week for pleasure.

Back when Andrew and I were writing our charter applications, I had contacted the English department chair at my kids' school to find out what would be on the assigned reading list. The curriculum consisted of only seven books a year. I called Andrew for help. "Could you send me a list of all the classics that a middle school kid should read?" I asked. He emailed me back a list of more than one hundred books that were not on the required school list. I posted his list in the kitchen on a bulletin board, purchased them all, and within a few years the kids had read just about all of them—for pleasure.

As I thought about how my kids' love of reading had empowered them to be intellectually curious and to readily do well in school, I decided to establish one goal for HVA: "Let's get all our kids to fall in love with reading!" I told the teachers that if our students really loved to read, they would naturally read at least an hour a day, and that would amount to about fifty books a year. But reading fifty books was not the goal, it was the measure of achieving it. The goal was to inspire students' love for reading.

Establishing that one simple goal tapped into our teachers' natural passion as educators and things began to take off.

Most of our HVA students told us that they had not read more than five or so books in any prior year. Their old schools did not get them into the habit of reading for pleasure. I'll never forget the twelve-year-old boy who admitted, "I used to throw my books away."

The challenge did not deter our teachers. They upgraded their classroom libraries, created exciting bulletin board displays, inspired students with motivational book talks, and improved lesson plans around pleasure reading. The reading teachers were on fire. And our principals were actively supporting them. Soon both schools were brimming with excitement about reading.

One of my favorite days at HVA came in the fall of our fourth year when I saw Eugene sitting on the floor in the auditorium inside during recess. He was engrossed in a book about football. I walked over and saw that he was hiding something. "What do you have there?" I asked. He didn't want me to see the book because he had scribbled notes about football all over the inside cover. Whether or not he should have been writing in a book was of no concern to me. He was reading at grade level—and he was reading and writing for pleasure.

Eugene looked at me with his incredible smile. "I read it three times!"

CHAPTER 13

PEOPLE AND CULTURE

THE PHONE RANG ON AN OVERCAST Thursday morning in April 2007. "Hello. I'm calling from the White House. The president would like to visit your school on Tuesday."

By the time a swarm of Secret Service agents descended on our middle school the next day, I was pretty confident our teachers weren't pranking me. The agents scouted all the exits, the basement, the roof, and the stairwells. In four days, President George W. Bush would tour our school and deliver a speech in our auditorium about education reform.

That Friday night, the only topic of conversation at our family dinner table was the president's visit. "You'll all come Tuesday, right?" I asked.

"No way, Mom," Avi, now a high school senior, said. "Why would I want to be in the same room with the president who got us into Iraq?" I had raised a household of liberals, so Avi would be a hard sell. Back in sixth grade, his teacher had assigned the children to write letters to the new president. "Congratulations on being elected," his letter began. "I wish you the best in your new position. But I do have a few suggestions. First of all, you may want to learn how to speak English." (The teacher mailed all of the sixth graders' letters except his.)

"It's not about this president," Rachel said to Avi. "It's the fact that he is visiting Mom's school."

I agreed with Rachel. For me, this visit had nothing to do with politics. It was about honoring our students and teachers.

"Yes, and some good can come of this," Chava chimed in. "Maybe the president will take a grammar class while he's there!"

"Guys, this isn't a referendum on his policies," I said.

"Okay, okay—I'll go," Avi agreed. "But I won't stand. And I won't clap."

It was the beginning of a very long weekend. The media onslaught was dizzying. During our first four years, I had routinely declined TV and newspaper requests. It seemed like a distraction from our work. For the same reason, I hadn't bothered to create a website. Now we had no choice: Dozens of reporters had been granted full access by the White House to visit our school on the day of the president's visit. Like it or not, we were now in the national spotlight.

On Tuesday morning when I arrived at school, the streets were blocked off, police were staged on every corner, and snipers were poised on our roof. Media trucks had parked on all the side streets, and a big crowd of journalists and neighbors had gathered outside. Bomb-sniffing dogs patrolled the auditorium. In the adjacent recreation room, several unfamiliar janitors carried mops in a way that made me realize they were Secret Service guys doing a pretty bad job of being undercover.

The auditorium quickly filled up, and at 9 a.m. sharp, the doors were locked. "At this point, nobody is allowed to enter or exit the building," somebody with an earpiece told me and seven others on the welcoming committee. The Secret Service escorted us to a back hallway where the president was set to arrive. "Five minutes!" one of the agents said.

Suddenly the Secret Service changed their plan and hurried everyone but me upstairs. I was left standing alone as motorcade sirens pierced the air and the presidential limo pulled into our blacktop playground. A dozen Secret Service agents quickly surrounded it. The president walked briskly toward me, and as I led him upstairs, he started asking me questions. "Why did you start this school? What do you think about testing? How do you get such great results?"

The school tour was scheduled to last twenty minutes but it turned into an hour because the president graciously visited every single classroom. "Boo!" he said, poking his head into classrooms that had not been on the official schedule, to the delight of students and teachers.

Then, before I knew it, I was standing in the glare of dozens of cameras in a packed auditorium making an introduction. "Ladies and gentlemen, the president of the United States."

That night, HVA was featured on every major television network. The president had hailed our school as a national model. "Schools everywhere should follow the example of Harlem Village Academies," he said. "I love coming to a place where people defy expectations." Mayor Michael Bloomberg called Harlem Village Academies "a national model of excellence." Before long, celebrities, politicians, educators, and CEOs would visit regularly. *NBC Nightly News* anchor Brian Williams later called us "a lesson for America's schools about what works."

A board member had called just after the evening news. "This is amazing!" he said. "Thanks," I replied, "but you know, it shouldn't be amazing. In my kids' school in Westchester most all the students pass the tests every year and nobody celebrates. It's just expected. What I really want to see is students writing sophisticated—"

"Deborah," he interrupted, "give me a break! You're being ridiculous. It was a great day. Just enjoy it."

Avi overheard our conversation. He had strong opinions about, well, everything. "Who were you talking to?" he asked. I told him someone had called to congratulate me, but I felt it was inappropriate for me to be in the spotlight when we still had so many areas that needed improvement.

"Mom, seriously? Why are you always like this? You reach ninety percent, but all you can see is the ten percent."

"He's right, Mom," Rachel said from the kitchen. "You should be happy."

I *was* happy for our students. They deserved to be acknowledged for their hard work. And I was happy to see the teachers and team recognized for their heroic accomplishments.

But the reality was that we hadn't yet actualized the founding vision of "a school for my children"—we weren't giving our students a private school quality education. We were all working incredibly hard, but we just weren't there yet. And I wasn't sure what to do to get us there.

In August, our teachers and principals would be gathering again for our fifth annual Summer Institute, and I'd have an opportunity to acknowledge the teachers' outstanding accomplishments. But what could I say to help all of us reconnect with the original vision? And, far more important, how could we fully execute on it?

The first morning of Institute, I arrived and saw something that I had never seen before at an HVA event: name tags. During our startup years, I had personally recruited every single teacher. Now we had so many new teachers that I hadn't even met them all.

I stepped to the podium and started off by expressing my genuine gratitude. "The whole country is astounded by what you have accomplished. And I am so proud of you," I said, singling out certain individuals and groups for well-deserved praise.

"The challenge now is to take our work to the next level. The world looks at our test scores and says we've closed the achievement gap. But we know better."

Then I told the teachers that I wanted them to keep three things in mind. First, I said, passing a state test doesn't mean we've closed the achievement gap. "We measure achievement by how well our students can analyze a sophisticated text, solve complex problems, write coherently, and *think* at a high level. We don't measure achievement by a basic test." Yes, I acknowledged, we are accountable for state test results every year, and we take that responsibility seriously. "But we want to teach above the test," I said. "Our children deserve that."

Second, we should not get too caught up in the headlines praising us for passing state tests. "I never used the word *pass* with my own children. Not once. And when I was growing up, I never heard the word *pass* in my home. There's really no place for that word in our schools. Think about what we expect of our own children. Would passing be good enough? Of course not."

Finally, I wanted to be clear that in my view academic achievement in itself is not enough. My educational vision was personal. "As a mother, what I want for my children is more than achievement, more than success," I said. "I want them to become wholesome in character, sophisticated intellectuals, fiercely independent thinkers, avid readers, and compassionate individuals who lead meaningful and reflective lives. And that's what I want for our children in Harlem."

I knew the teachers and I shared that vision. The question for me was what I could do to better support them as they tried to realize that ideal. When I observed instruction in our schools, I'd see some classes that were outstanding, and others were good, but some were mediocre. This variation was not okay with me.

Often, I went out to dinner to talk with teachers and principals.

Some of the teachers were happy, while others expressed serious frustration. Many teachers energized the teachers' office with positivity, came up with ideas, and took initiative to solve problems at "our" schools, but others complained about "the" schools and brought down morale with negativity, drama, or gossip.

Then there were the students. Virtually all our students appreciated how much their teachers cared about them. But some students dropped by my office to tell me that they were unhappy, that too many classes were not great, or that "school is boring."

Compared to most public schools we were seen as a national model. By the end of our fifth year our students made history as the first class ever in Harlem to achieve 100 percent proficiency in eighth-grade math. But our national acclaim wasn't my focus. I was more concerned with what was happening on the ground: in the classrooms and teachers' offices. We attracted great teachers each year, but a lot of them became frustrated, and many left. I wanted to figure out what I could do better so that every single teacher in every classroom in every one of our schools would be happy and effective. I wanted *all* our teachers to reach their fullest potential, so that our students would do the same.

I had a lot of balls in the air: overseeing the quality of instruction, teacher recruiting, operations, literacy, fundraising, and other projects— all while we were opening our new high school in a temporary space. So we now had three schools: two fully enrolled middle schools and a new high school.

Back in our fourth year, the question of whether to start the high school had been an intense debate. If we did open a high school, it would be an enormous undertaking with a whole new set of challenges. But if we didn't open a high school, our eighth graders—the kids from our pioneer class—would be back in the very system that had served them so poorly before.

It had been a huge dilemma. So I did what I'd always done when

I had to make an important decision: gathered our leadership team. Nick, Laurie, Matt, my chief of staff, and a new academic director all crammed into my office, which I shared with four others. We sat around a small IKEA table to discuss the issue. "Don't breathe or the table will move!" Matt joked.

For what seemed like forever, we sat there discussing the pros and cons of opening the high school now. I listened to my colleagues articulate their positions. The argument to postpone was very strong. We had no facility and no high school experience. Then there was the very real tension between quality and growth. Isn't it better to focus our time and energy on our two schools rather than open a third school?

"Deborah, it's sweltering in here. Open a damn window!" Nick said.

As I slid by to open the office window I glanced outside and saw Rayisha, an eighth grader, on the playground. I was so fond of this child and she'd come so far in three years. How could we let her down? How could we take a risk with her future? Suddenly the debate was no longer philosophical or practical. For me, it was about Rayisha.

We took a vote. Two were in favor and two were against. I was the tiebreaker.

Now we needed a permanent high school building. Although I'd dealt with facilities issues back when we renovated temporary space for our first school, I was hardly prepared for how unbelievably difficult it would be to build an actual school building in New York City: driving through the streets of Harlem in a van to scout out a location, convincing a seller who had turned down many other offers to accept ours, attending community board meetings to garner support, dealing with opposition, fighting layers of bureaucracy, and persuading elected officials. Thank goodness we had advisors with real-estate

194 | BORN TO RISE

expertise to guide us through the complicated legal, architectural, financial, and logistical issues. I later joked with friends about how the agonizing process of building a facility had made me cry at least three times.

The first time was when the original seller told me at a meeting in his midtown office that he had decided to take his property off the market, despite the fact that I'd worked on that deal for eighteen months. The newsstand operator on the corner of Fifty-Seventh and Seventh was very kind as he sold me a packet of tissues.

The second time was the day our second facility deal was denied by a state regulator after two years of meetings and hundreds of phone calls. I burst into tears. Then I threw on my sneakers and started running as fast as I could. Eight months and dozens of meetings later, it was finally approved. But we still had to raise the funds.

And the third time was when the global financial markets crashed in 2008, and our largest funder withdrew support at the last minute, leaving us with just five weeks to raise millions of dollars or lose the entire project.

Back in 2002, at the Gates conference in Providence, Don and Larry had tried to warn me. Running an educational startup would be nonstop—and it would be just as much about business, finance, fundraising, governance, and facilities as it was about academics. How right they were.

So despite the day-to-day challenges, I made it a priority to set aside a little time to talk with CEOs whom I'd met through my fundraising efforts. After all, they too had to manage a team, plan for growth, balance short-term problems with longer-term strategy, and deliver results. I was always looking to learn more about how I could become a better leader and improve our organization.

As I told one CEO about my interest in improving the quality of instruction across all of our schools, he shifted the discussion: "I'm more interested in your organization's values than your performance, because it's your values that drive your performance." He pointed out that I hadn't really engaged my leadership team in a discussion of values. Another CEO showed me his company's values and culture statement and talked about it at length. He took his corporate values personally, and even used them to reflect on his own leadership weaknesses each year. He suggested that I create a statement of my own. I had seen these before, but they always seemed to be just for show, a document on a company website that made your eyes glaze over. How would articulating our values impact our results?

At the next lunch I had with a corporate leader I asked about his management philosophy. "It's people and culture—all the results follow from there," he said.

"You hire people you trust completely to do the job. Then you create a culture that enables them to do their best work. That's it. You have to appreciate and support people, and take away the roadblocks so they can do their job. But you know this already," he said.

Perhaps I did. I had written about many of these things in our original business plan. And we had done a lot of it well in our first five years, like empowering and supporting teachers. But still, there was something missing in my execution.

Then I asked a question so basic it was almost embarrassing: "What do you mean when you say culture?"

"Culture is about how people feel at work," he said, "and it's how you treat people. I insist that people treat each other the way they would want to be treated. When people feel good at work, when people are really happy, they do their best work."

As simple as it sounded, something about those words clicked on a gut level. *When people are really happy, they do their best work.* Culture is about how people *feel at work.*

I had been missing it all along. Culture is about how people *feel at work.* I had been leading with my head, sharing my best thinking, connecting to my team on an intellectual level based on our passion for education. But I hadn't understood how my words and actions made people feel each day, and how their feelings affected the quality of their work. Drucker had talked about "attitude" as essential to knowledge worker productivity, but I hadn't fully understood it until this moment.

I came away from that lunch with clarity and conviction. The conversation led me to ask myself a series of questions about people and culture: Did we have exactly the right person in every key job in our organization? We did not. Did I always treat people the way I would want to be treated? I did not. Did we have an optimal workplace culture throughout all our schools? No. How could we develop a culture that enabled all our teachers to do their best work? I wasn't yet sure.

What I *was* sure about was this: if I wanted to improve our organization, I first had to improve myself. So I started reflecting on my own leadership based on the insights from that lunch. Specifically, I started to reflect on culture, on how I made people feel at work.

First, I realized that I had to stop wanting everything to be perfect. My lack of patience was not just with mediocrity—it was with anything other than excellence. When I thought about how I looked at my own tasks, I was never interested in what I had accomplished; all I cared about was what was not going well so I could fix it. This outlook didn't feel negative to me. But in retrospect it was obvious that focusing on what was not working just made people feel discouraged. On one level, high standards and a sense of urgency were important. As my longtime chief of staff, Matt, once said, "Your relentless pursuit of excellence is embedded in our organizational DNA—it's why we get results." But it also caused stress to those around me. It wasn't that I had to lower my standards, but I did have to be more patient and not expect perfection.

I had made other mistakes during our startup years, but one of the most significant was that I had only fully trusted a few rock stars—our master teachers. Trusting rock stars was easy; I never micromanaged

Nick as a math teacher or Rebecca as a reading teacher. What was harder—what I hadn't done—was to understand and cultivate the full potential in every teacher. The teachers appreciated my passion for every aspect of education, but I should have focused more on bringing out *their* passion. While I did empower teachers to make decisions, my first impulse had been to research the best way to do something and share all that I knew. Sometimes this helped people who worked closely with me and we got amazing results together. But I had overlooked the importance of people taking complete ownership and figuring things out for themselves. My own most significant learning had come through doing my work and learning from my mistakes; I needed to give others the same opportunity. If I had, perhaps a lot more of our teachers in those early years would have felt happier and would have stayed.

Another insight came to me as I thought back to a conversation with Nick at a leadership retreat in our fourth year. In a quiet moment during one of our breaks, he had asked me if my nonstop intensity was a way of blocking out the pain of losing Joel. I could have replied, "No, I've been a workaholic since I was twelve," which was true. But I did wonder if easing up would have left me with time to feel the guilt that I had carried with me. I had never gotten over the feeling that it should have been me instead of Joel. He didn't get to have his life, yet I did. It wasn't fair. Why should I get to be happy? I thought of the poem Rachel wrote when she was eight years old: "Life was so fun, but now it's so dim." And I realized that Nick was right, that my spirit had been so depleted when Joel died that I had kind of shut off my feelings in order to function each day. I had lost my natural sense of fun and happiness. Without any awareness of the impact of my actions, I was making other people around me less happy. For example, I would start meetings by immediately jumping into the first agenda item without even taking a few minutes to enjoy the company of my colleagues or ask how they were doing.

During his final year, Joel had made me a painting that I'd framed. I had put it up on the wall of my office along with the words of Aeschylus that I'd often read: "He who learns must suffer, / And even in our sleep pain that cannot forget, / Falls drop by drop upon the heart, / And in our own despair, against our will, / Comes wisdom to us by the awful grace of God." If I continued to exude a constant sense of sacrifice and guilt, everyone around me would feel less happy and our organizational culture would be diminished. I had to let myself go back to being myself. I had to let myself be happy and have fun so everyone around me could do the same.

Why had it taken me so long to grasp all this?

I decided that "people and culture" would be the topic of our next leadership team retreat, which we held each year at the very end of June, after the last day of school. In previous years, the topics had always been educational matters, such as literacy or learning standards. The first person I turned to for help with our culture-themed leadership retreat was Laurie, who had joined us back in our third year as principal of our second middle school. We worked together: I crafted a first draft of our culture and values statement while she created our retreat agenda.

When she had started as principal, I noticed right away that Laurie was a brilliant leader with pitch-perfect instincts for bringing out the best in each person. To help Laurie start our second school, I had asked Yohana and Rebecca to join her team: as dean and writing teacher, respectively. They both loved working with Laurie.

Laurie also had a special gift for relationships with students, which had taken our entire behavior system to a whole new level. Her approach was a great balance of warmth, fun, and strictness that eventually made its way into all our classrooms. She joked with kids, while still commanding respect and maintaining order. As time went on, I paid increasing attention to her talent. All the things that I had struggled to learn came naturally to her. I knew she'd be exactly the right person to develop a plan for our first-ever culture leadership retreat.

On June 29, when we arrived at the lodge in upstate New York, everyone was delighted—and a bit surprised—to find that I had added time for a break from 1 to 3 p.m. I'd written on the agenda: "Nap. Hike. Whatevs." Amazingly, it had never occurred to me before to make time for fun and relaxation during our retreats.

I'd brought the rough draft of the culture and values document to our first session, and we spent all day debating, discussing, and refining each point.

By the end of the day, we had articulated thirteen values that reflected what we aspired to be, what we believed, what we expected from ourselves and our teachers.

This was not just a piece of paper. It would soon become the heart and soul of our culture.

OUR CULTURE—OUR VALUES
HARLEM VILLAGE ACADEMIES

A CULTURE OF TEAM

Children come first. We put children's needs before our own. The well-being and achievement of children is our highest priority, and all our decisions are based on what's best for them.

Team before individual. Being a team means helping others and going the extra mile to contribute to the group, rather than seeking the limelight. It's working with people who share our values, and our desire to live a meaningful life dedicated to the greater good. It's about humility and being loyal to people.

We revere teachers. Schools should be designed to respect, nurture, develop, trust, and support teachers. The most revered individuals in our community are master teachers, as we profoundly respect a lifelong teaching career. We work tirelessly to support teachers in every way possible.

We radiate positivity. We energize each other with positive talk, attitudes, and actions. We don't tolerate even a little negativity, complaining, arrogance, divisiveness, or gossip—it does not bring sunshine to our day.

It's a love fest in our love nest! There are many ways we express our love: through acts of kindness, support, and appreciation. We hire people we really like, and we enjoy close relationships. Even when we're frustrated or tired, we insist on treating each other as we would want to be treated.

Can you hear me now? Real communication happens here—and the most important part is listening. So much good comes from listening and understanding one another. With our hearts in the right place, we assume the best of one another. We work through disagreements and difficult situations. So put down the headphones, get off email, and walk down the hall or pick up the phone for a real conversation.

We want to have fun, damn it! We spend a lot of time together so we make it fun. We're idealists but we also work too hard to not bubble-wrap a colleague's desk once in a while.

A CULTURE OF OWNERSHIP

We love what we do! We are passionate and driven. We work for social justice with seriousness and a sense of urgency. We run to meetings. We are resilient even in times of stress, because our work is a sacred calling.

We hold ourselves accountable for results. We take pride in personal accountability for the achievement of our students. We feel accountable to our children, and we feel accountable to each other. We are accountable as individuals and as a team. We do not believe in blame or excuses, just results and hard work.

We're continually improving. Everyone is entrusted to practice *kaizen:* to continually improve everything, every day. We are relentless about excellence and can't stand mediocrity. We take initiative and share ideas. This is our school. We are empowered and dedicated to make it the best it can be every day.

If we ever become a bureaucracy, please shoot us. Everyone here is an entrepreneur. We banish roadblocks and minimize bureaucratic non-sense. When a problem arises, we figure out a solution—and implement it quickly. We live for people with a work ethic who execute well and get the job done.

A CULTURE OF LEARNING

We're continually learning. We always push ourselves to learn and grow. We invest the time and effort to support our own and each other's development.

Kounaikenshuu is at the heart of our professional development philosophy: we plan together, observe and analyze each other's lessons, and collaborate to refine teaching strategies and continuously improve student learning. We talk all the time about teaching. The intellectual energy is palpable!

Words that define us . . . Passion. Hope. Love. Fun. Team. Humility. Leaders. Meritocracy. Idealism. Kindness. Activists.

Words that make us cringe . . . Mediocrity. Bureaucracy. Gossip. Intolerance. Arrogance. Divisiveness. Blame. Complain. Apathy.

Working together to develop our values was an incredible experience that brought us even closer to each other, if that was possible.

We immediately began to see ways in which our culture and values document would help us in the future as we grew our organization. It would help us communicate what we were about when hiring. It would give us a common language to understand what we were working toward as we coached and evaluated teachers. It would help us to improve ourselves as leaders.

Most significant of all, the process itself somehow instilled in us a profound appreciation of that one core idea about organizational leadership: *It's people and culture—all results follow from there.*

After dinner our first day, we sat around the lodge and gabbed. Even though we were tired, nobody wanted to go to sleep. It was fun to just hang out. I mentioned that the lodge reminded me of the old buildings at my summer camp, which reminded me of something we used to do: staying up half the night singing old TV sitcom theme songs. From *Gilligan's Island* and *The Brady Bunch* to our favorite, *The Mary Tyler Moore Show*, I knew almost every one by heart, as did Mary, a writing teacher who had recently become an academic director. Once we started singing, we couldn't stop. "No, really," Sam and Matt said, covering their ears. "Enough. Stop." To which Mary and I responded: "You guys know you love it! Awesome! We'll keep going!"

When I was a camp counselor, I loved the people I worked with. I experienced what it meant to be part of a great team—to work with smart idealists interested in changing the world. My dream was that this would last my whole life.

I felt the same with these colleagues, whom I adored. It was as if I were back at camp as a twenty-two-year-old counselor: The laughter and friendship, the depth of our mutual trust, which enabled us to get through hard times when we were really frustrated with one another, and the intellectual stimulation of being among such brilliant minds. As someone said at one of our dinners, "I feel sorry for everyone who's not us."

The leadership retreat had left me on a high, but this was the summer I had been dreading for years. Rachel, my youngest, was about to leave for college. Now all three kids would be out of the house and I didn't want to stay there alone. And despite occasional dating, I still hadn't met anyone special while living in the suburbs. So I decided to move back to New York City.

The kids loved the idea. "This will be great for you, Mom," Rachel said, sweetly. "You can go to lectures and yoga classes, and maybe you'll meet someone." Chava agreed: "You know, Mom, your theory that someone will just appear in your life has not quite worked out. So you're going to have to make an effort." I told her that I knew she was right but I secretly held on to my "it will just happen" plan. Besides, I was so busy I didn't have time to think about it.

Moving into the city would be a great adventure, but packing up and searching for an apartment was a huge undertaking, especially since I had less than a month until the teachers would return for our annual Summer Institute. So I decided to look for an apartment over the Fourth of July weekend, knowing that everyone else would be at the beach. I went online and found a place that met my three criteria: safe location, near a gym, and close to Harlem. On July 3, I drove into the city with Chava and met with the Realtor, and by July 5 I had signed a three-year lease. No more commuting!

The kids took summer jobs and on the weekends, they helped me pack. We had so much stuff to give away that I called Big Brothers Big Sisters to send a truck. Even with that, I was moving from a house to a one-bedroom apartment, so we had to store lots of boxes in my parents' basement. I asked the kids to carefully label the boxes so we'd be able to find things later, but Avi didn't see the point. When I lost my patience and told him to "just do what I ask" he seemed to acquiesce. Only later did I discover that he'd labeled boxes "random crap" and "other random crap."

The day before the movers arrived, I walked through the empty house. We had moved to Westchester when the kids were just starting elementary school. I remember their teachers that first year: Rachel had Ms. Tucci for kindergarten, Chava had Ms. Lane, and Avi had Ms. Savarese. How did the time go by so fast?

I looked through the kitchen window at the front driveway, where they had carved pumpkins, set up lemonade stands, and helped Joel restore his old Mustangs. In the backyard they'd built a tree house, played hide-and-seek with Avi's best friend, Eric, and jumped in the autumn leaves with the neighborhood kids. And I was really going to miss those beautiful pink flowers that bloomed on our cherry trees every spring.

I had woken up that morning in the town where all three kids had spent their entire childhood. By the end of the day I was back in the city where they had all been born. The move had exhausted me, but I was so anxious to unpack that I just kept opening boxes when the kids and I got to the apartment. By 9 p.m., my head was pounding. "Mom, you have to lie down. We'll unpack; you've done enough. I'll do the bedroom stuff," said Chava, who was always so thoughtful. Rachel organized the entire kitchen. And Avi, who was standing amid forty boxes of books, started putting them on shelves.

We had a new, oversized sofa bed in the living room that would double as the kids' summer bedroom. I had bought it at Rebecca's recommendation; she had one just like it in her new apartment in Brooklyn. At night the girls slept on the sofa, and Avi sprawled on an air mattress on the floor. When the sofa was opened up, all four of us could lie down and still have room for popcorn and all of our laptops. We called it "the boat" because it was so huge. We hung out on the boat together watching movies or reading for hours. We were cramped, but happy as clams.

With just a few weeks until college, the kids enjoyed city life. Rachel ran in Central Park while Chava took up Bikram yoga and Avi took up meditation. The girls explored SoHo and sometimes joined Avi, who spent almost every night reading, writing, and drinking chai tea at Barnes & Noble until it closed at eleven.

One Sunday afternoon in August, I drove upstate to my old summer camp for a very special occasion: a reunion and tribute to Mel Reisfeld. I was overcome with a mixture of delight and longing as I walked around the camp where I had grown up, where I'd had the time of my life.

My friends Ronnie and Steve and I each spoke in honor of Mel's decades of service. "Learning from Mel was like nothing most of us had ever done before," Ronnie said. "He inspired us and kept things interesting with what we'd now call politically incorrect comments. He worked with each group of kids as if they were his first and we only found out later that he told each of us that we were his favorite."

A professor from the University of Pennsylvania said, "I've been teaching for forty years but I can still remember the things I learned from Mel. He educated the educators."

Steve called Mel the "man of the century" and proceeded to lead everyone in singing a song that he had written about him.

When it was my turn to speak, I looked over and saw Mel sitting with that same spark in his eye. "Mel instilled in us a passion for learning and for wanting to change the world," I said. "I speak on behalf of all of us when I say thank you, Mel: we will never be able to repay you for what you did for us."

Mel stood up and started to take a little piece of paper out of his pocket. He looked at the paper, then looked at us. "Guys, I'm just about to cry," he said, "but I never used notes before so I won't now!"

Everyone clapped and cheered as he folded up the paper and stuffed it back into his pocket. Then he looked at all of us.

"I had a calling—teaching—and I've been doing it for fifty years," he said. "You are continuing the legacy of learning and caring and social activism." Mel told us to look around at the camp. I looked around: There was the dining hall where Karen and I talked for hours, there was the apple tree where Sara and I planned our fifth-grade curriculum when we were counselors, there was the cabin that Jon and his friends had wrapped in toilet paper at midnight, there was the staff house where I skipped out of a lecture to listen to Steve play guitar all night. I had made my lifelong best friends here. And I had learned to be a rule breaker and an activist. "Every tree, every little nook and cranny reminds you of some adventure we've had," Mel said. "And my adventure has been half a century. And I have loved it. And I love all of you."

As if that afternoon weren't enough to get me emotional, the very next week it was time for all three of my kids to go off to college. Chava was the first to leave, and I started crying as they all knew I would. "Mom, don't be sad," Avi said. "She's annoying anyway." Then before long it was his turn to leave, and finally it would be my youngest, Rachel's, turn. As I helped her unpack and move into her freshman dorm, Rachel suggested I adopt a baby. "You need another child!" In fact, I would soon have many more children as we had started planning for the launch of our new elementary schools.

Traveling back to New York, I was sure that I'd be depressed; it was just a question of how depressed and for how many months. I would be returning to a quiet, dark apartment. The nest would be completely empty for the first time in twenty-one years.

The elevator door opened and I walked down the hall to my new apartment. I opened the door, stepped inside, and walked straight to the window. As I looked out at the city skyline, I felt . . . surprisingly happy. I was excited for the year ahead, the important work ahead, my new life.

CHAPTER 14

SCENES FROM
A REVOLUTION

I KEPT THINKING ABOUT THAT ADVICE I had heard: if you focus on people and culture, the results will follow. Culture became my first priority, and before I knew it, I was spending a lot of my time talking about it—and working on it—with our school principals. I convened another leadership retreat where we brainstormed everything we could come up with to make teachers happy. We met with grade team leaders to reflect on how to improve our schools by focusing on culture. We started explicitly talking about values with teachers.

I had written in our business plan back in 2001: "Most people possess enormous talent and potential that lies dormant in organizations that don't know how to ignite it." Finally after all these years, we had figured it out. Our teachers became their best selves once we learned how to develop a culture that brought out the passion and best performance in each person.

And what it had ultimately come down to was our three aspects of culture: teamwork, learning, and ownership.

It was 10 a.m. on a Wednesday, and Justin, an experienced eighth-grade teacher, had just finished teaching a history lesson. As he walked down the hall toward the teachers' office, he peered through the windows of a few classrooms. He wanted to keep an eye out in case any new teachers needed help.

The first few looked fine, but Justin stopped in his tracks when he got to Rutgers, a seventh-grade classroom. Just as Jane, a new teacher, turned her back to the class, a student threw a piece of an eraser toward the front of the room. When it landed, Justin noticed there were about ten other bright pink eraser tips scattered on the floor. Knowing he needed to act quickly, Justin practically ran to the teachers' office, where Lisa, the principal, was meeting with another teacher, Ariella. He quickly explained what was happening in Jane's room. "We need everyone who's available to help," Ariella said to the other teachers, all of whom had just settled in for their prep time. With that, every single teacher—nine in all—got up and marched together toward Rutgers. They were like a huge wall of people walking down the hall. "It felt like a superhero movie," Lisa said, "and the amazing thing was that the teachers all wanted to help even though they didn't know yet what the problem was."

Suddenly, to the students' surprise, fourteen adults walked in and stood around the perimeter of the classroom.

The enrichment director, Ajua, stood at the front of the room. "Who knows about the erasers being thrown?" she asked.

All of the students slowly raised their hands.

She stood silently for a moment, letting her look of disappointment sink in. Then she said, "Now raise your hand if you threw an eraser." More than half the kids raised their hands.

"Why would you do that? And why didn't anyone say something to try and stop it?" she asked. The students were silent.

"Does anyone have anything to say?" The students were still silent as fourteen pairs of adult eyes stared at them. "There are erasers all over the floor now. Your teachers and I spend a lot of time decorating your classrooms and keeping them clean. We want them to look nice for you. And you made it a mess."

One girl raised her hand. "I want to apologize," her voice choked up. "It was wrong." Three other students lowered their eyes while she was talking.

"So how do we fix this?" Justin asked, stepping to the front of the room.

"We could clean the classroom," one boy offered. Another suggested that they could each write an apology letter to the teacher.

In the very back a student raised her hand. When Justin called on her, all the other students looked at her. "I'm sorry we lost your trust," she said.

Jane was moved by the experience. "Classroom management isn't my forte, but nobody was judging me," she said. "It was so supportive. It made me feel motivated."

The way teachers support each other is central to our culture of team. But there's more to it: On the deepest level our culture of team is about putting each other's needs before our own. And children's needs before everything. Much like the unconditional love that is part of being a family, when you put the other's needs first, you each receive more in return.

Our culture of team ultimately impacts the students, because children learn best from the examples of the adults around them. A visitor commented that he had never in his life seen middle school students showing so much kindness to one another. "I think it's because they can tell we're all a little bit in love with each other," a special education teacher said.

Our team culture is also about having fun. We hang out with each other at weekend football games and Friday happy hours. And most of us will never forget the time our new principal, Sam, received a package covered in bubble wrap and decided to put it to good use: bubble-wrapping a teacher's desk, chair, computer, and keyboard.

And team is most definitely about being thoughtful: refraining from gossip and always assuming the best of others. We put the highest premium on treating each other the way we would want to be treated.

I learned from Laurie that creating a team culture starts with figuring out what each person is passionate about, and honoring that by giving each person a chance to shine. One teacher may be the absolute best at handling conversations with parents, another at creating effective schedules, another at motivating struggling students. When everyone contributes in his or her own way, it sparks an energy that can only be described as magical and then the whole—the team—is greater than the sum of its parts.

As the effect of culture has become more clear to us over time, we've learned how important it is to protect it. Indeed, the culture can be threatened by just one person who shows disregard for our shared values. Sometimes the only option is to part ways. One teacher we hired delivered great test scores, but she didn't embrace our deeply held value that all children can learn. She even told certain students not to bother taking the Regents exam because they would never pass. Her attitude made several colleagues angry and created tension on the team. We had to ask her to leave, although we gave her plenty of time to find another position. But that lesson stuck with all of us: when even one person is misaligned with values, it can hurt the entire team.

Culture is a fragile ecosystem. It is impossible to nurture a positive culture without the right to hire and fire at will, and to do so freely based not just on performance but also on values. Leaders need to be completely free to build teams of people who are committed to our shared values and will support one another.

My graduation from
nursery school

My family

With friends at summer camp—
I'm at the top left

Freshman year of college

Our three kids on their first day of school

Joel playing guitar

Joel with the kids on top of one
of his restored Mustangs

Avi with the "Welcome Home Daddy"
signs he and the girls made when Joel
was in the hospital

Being a single mom—ballet and karate on
Saturday afternoons (Rachel making a funny
face!)

At Sesame Street

Collating the charter application—my three
kids and my son's best friend

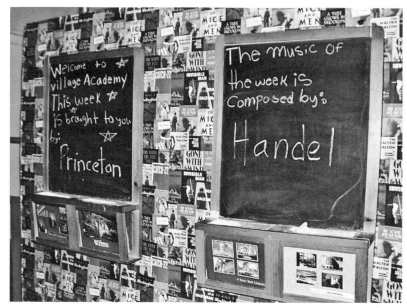

Bulletin boards warmly welcome students and families on the very first day of our first year

Rebecca teaching

Nick tutoring

In addition to required classics, students select and read fifty books each year for pleasure

Nick and Rebecca working in the teachers' office

Yohana with a student

The first annual HVA family picnic—my daughters are on the right

Potato sack races

Mary in the classroom

Laurie working with a student at our second school

Student–teacher football game

On the playground at recess

In the first weeks of school, our new fifth graders learn about our behavior expectations

Students spend thirty minutes a day reading for pleasure during school

Science experiments

Orderly hallway rules make middle school students feel safe

Writing class

Nitin teaching sixth grade math

Our kids enjoy fun school trips like ice skating throughout the year

Choir practice at our after-school program "Find Your Passion"

Playing chess at "Find Your Passion"

Each school plans a social event for teachers; here it's karaoke

The leadership team goofing around during a break at retreat

Dressed up as a hippie witch at our staff Halloween party

Teachers at our annual Summer Institute

Teachers collaborating to continually
improve the curriculum

At the construction site of our
new high school on 125th Street

The most important teacher in my life: Mel

Camp friend Ron and me speaking at the tribute in Mel's honor

The first graduating class—my babies—off to college!

Essence magazine founder Ed Lewis was our commencement speaker at the first graduation of Harlem Village Academies

Left to right: Chava, me, Avi, and Rachel—the nest
is empty, but the birds come back in the summer!

Perhaps most important of all, our team culture is defined by a sense of connectedness, a transcendent bond with others that comes from dedication to a cause greater than oneself.

Like many of our teachers, Peter had been in a traditional city public school before coming to Harlem Village Academies. There, his professional development consisted of occasional training workshops. "They were somewhat helpful," Peter says, "but they didn't really change the quality of my teaching."

When he got to HVA, he saw that our approach to developing him would be completely different. So different, in fact, that when he heard about it he was skeptical.

Our approach to professional development is based on the Japanese practice of *kounaikenshuu*, in which teachers collaborate to continually improve of all aspects of the school. One type of *kounaikenshuu* is called lesson study: teachers plan one lesson together, observe each other teaching, analyze the outcome, and then refine the lesson and teach it again.

"I didn't see the point of spending a full school year working on just one lesson with four other math teachers," Peter admitted. But he gave it a try.

Peter's group selected a research theme: teaching students to solve problems independently. Next they selected a specific objective for the lesson: students will be able to multiply binomials. "I was sitting there thinking: I already know how to teach this," Peter said. But as he soon discovered, each teacher had a different approach. Not only that, the process of discussing the lesson in such detail "pushed me to see things I hadn't seen before about how to improve my teaching." Peter and the other math teachers met regularly to discuss this one specific lesson.

Finally, in March, Peter taught the lesson for the first time with a half dozen other teachers observing. "It was nerve-racking. The lesson did not go very well." That afternoon, his team met to review the feedback they had received from the observing teachers, and they made a lot of changes to the lesson based on the discussion.

A month later, the revised lesson was taught again, this time with twenty teachers, both from our schools and from other schools across the country observing and giving Peter feedback.

"Lesson study completely transformed the way I teach," Peter says, "I used to deliver information to students about mathematical formulas: some of them got it, others didn't. Now I facilitate a process where they have to do the work of discovering and understanding the concepts so deeply that they are able to devise the formulas."

After 100 percent of his students scored proficient on the state test, they told us the test was so much easier than their class work. Peter was becoming a rock star before my very eyes. His sophisticated teaching reminded me of Rebecca and Nick when I first met them. The only difference was that back then, I had assumed they were naturals. It turned out that wasn't the case. "In my first few years," Rebecca said, "I didn't know how to teach kids to read. My instruction had a lot of fluff and not much substance." Nick said the same thing. "I had good relationships and kept the kids busy, but my instruction was not high level. I didn't know what I was doing."

Both of them had *become* rock stars after years of devoting several hours each week to learning and developing themselves. Nick was in weekly lesson study and Rebecca was in a literacy study group where she analyzed videotapes of her lessons with colleagues. For years, they read and discussed professional literature and received guidance from experienced teachers. And arguably the most important part of their development, they both told me, was the time and care they put into lesson planning. "There is no way to be a good teacher without planning a purposeful approach to every lesson," said Rebecca.

A culture of learning in an adult workplace is not just about "training." A culture of learning is when a community of knowledge workers is empowered and inspired to continually learn and develop as professionals.

People learn best by actually doing their work, making mistakes, and collaborating to improve their own practice. It's an upward spiral: the teachers get better every year as the curriculum gets better, each causing and caused by the other.

On a hot Saturday back in June 2004, I had brought my three kids to the Modell's sporting goods store in Yonkers. They needed new sneakers for summer camp. As we walked downstairs to the shoe department, I spotted Mrs. Swanson, whose son, Emmanuel, had not passed fifth grade. Emmanuel was one of the sweetest boys in the school. He was also one of our lowest-level readers, having entered fifth grade at a kindergarten reading level. Even though he had progressed to a second-grade level over the course of the year, he would need one more year to catch up on his reading skills.

I said hello to Mrs. Swanson and started chatting. Within minutes she told me that she was pulling her son from our school. I loved Emmanuel! So did all the teachers. We had all become attached to him, as we had to all of our kids. I tried convincing Mrs. Swanson to stay, explaining that HVA was superior to the neighborhood school that was willing to take him in as a sixth grader. He'd be better off in the long run if he caught up on reading now. She was polite but unmoved by my protestations. After a while, my kids became impatient. "Mommmmm," they whispered, "we really want to go."

I never saw Emmanuel again. It was heartbreaking.

Unfortunately, this story repeated itself many times. It would take us years to figure out how to keep so many of our struggling students from giving up and leaving.

We lost all kinds of kids for all kinds of reasons. Our first valedictorian moved to Florida. A gifted violinist found a school she preferred closer to her home. Several boys left for schools with better sports programs. But our biggest problem continued to be losing students who were struggling with academics.

Yolinda was another one of the many children we lost before we finally figured out how to be more proactive about the issue. She struggled in all her subjects, especially math. While her classmates mastered addition in three weeks, it took Yolinda three months. By Thanksgiving most of our fifth graders had learned their basic math facts—addition, subtraction, multiplication, and division—but it took Yolinda all year to learn these basics. By June she had failed all her classes, and her math grade was an abysmal 40 percent. All of Yolinda's teachers agreed: it was imperative for her to repeat fifth grade. As with Emmanuel, if we didn't hold Yolinda back, she would be set up to fail in the upper grades, too.

Yolinda's teachers suspected that she had a learning disability, but her mother refused to allow us to evaluate her; she felt that the label "special education" would be a stigma. Ironically, in so many other cases, we had sought to *de*classify students whom we believed had been erroneously labeled special education. With Yolinda, we gave her the tutoring she needed despite the lack of an official designation.

Teacher after teacher tried to help. "I visited her at home three times," said one. "I tutored her every day at lunch," said another. Despite all this effort, she did not pass her core subjects and would need to repeat the grade. But her mother was adamantly against it and pulled her from the school. What could we do?

Sam and his teachers decided that one of their school goals for the next year would be this: No More Yolindas. Before long, the teachers had developed a plan. As I watched their process unfold, I was struck by the fact that the teachers did not think of themselves as solving "the attrition problem"—not once did I hear them talk about our statistics.

Their interest was personal—it was about helping the kids and keeping them with us so we could educate them for the long term. Those teachers loved Yolinda as much as I had loved Emmanuel, and they knew that staying in our school could be a life-changing difference for a child.

The teachers came up with ideas to improve everything from tutoring and behavior systems to parent communication. In the past parents had only heard the "bad news" in the spring, and they had chosen to leave rather than allow their child to be held back. The improved plan was to communicate with parents far in advance: "Your child is starting with us at a first-grade level. We will do whatever it takes to catch him up but it's simply impossible to move a child five grade levels in one year. We need two years." Then Sam and the deans would assure the children, "You are very smart, but your prior school did not prepare you properly." These early discussions made all the difference.

What ultimately reduced our student attrition so dramatically? It was the teachers' ownership of the situation. "We didn't have to make a proposal and wait a week to get approval," one of our math teachers Steve later said to me. "We had ideas to help the students and we just did it."

A culture of ownership allows teachers to be their best. We trust our teachers to make decisions at every level: at workout and in grade team meetings and individually. We give them the freedom to design or select their curriculum, even to choose their own paths toward professional development. And they know that with trust comes responsibility: they are accountable to deliver results.

Our culture of ownership is as genuine as it is powerful.

Steve said that he personally knew of at least twelve students who would have failed that year if the teachers had not been able to move quickly and effectively. "We came up with a plan and we knew it would be okay to run with it, because our plan was consistent with our values."

And one of our seventh-grade reading teachers, David, said our culture of ownership brought out his passion. "It was exhilarating to be trusted and empowered. It made me feel I could be the kind of teacher I had always dreamed about becoming: funny, interesting, creative, energetic."

I was beginning to feel a revolution starting. One led by the teachers themselves.

CHAPTER 15

BE THE CULTURE

CULTURE IS HOW A PLACE FEELS and how it makes people feel.

After many discussions both inside and outside our organization, I had come to understand that culture is so critical because it determines whether people will do their best work.

A great culture brings out each person's highest potential—and an amazing culture transforms people.

We were constantly asking our teachers, both informally and during formal feedback sessions: what more can we do to make you happy? Most of the teachers really appreciated all the effort. They gave us feedback and we did our best to act on it. They certainly knew how sincerely the school leaders and I cared about them.

Then one day I got an email from Liz, a sixth-grade writing teacher with extraordinarily positive energy. "I've been thinking . . ." it started. Liz and I had been talking informally about culture all year. She had a thought that she wanted to share, so we decided to meet for lunch during summer vacation. We ordered in salads and I told her that I was intent on figuring out how to fully actualize that workplace nirvana I had been seeking. I was sure it could be done. Liz felt the same way.

What she said next completely changed the way I thought about organizational culture.

Why, Liz asked, had I made it my job to create a great workplace culture? "Everyone knows how much you respect teachers. Everyone knows how genuine you are when you say that you want us to be happy and empowered," she said, "but by asking teachers what more *you*, as the CEO, and the principals can do for *us*, maybe that puts the teachers into a passive role—like we are the receivers of the culture. I think we each have to take more responsibility to create the culture."

I think Liz saw the Aha! moment flash across my face.

I had given teachers ownership over curriculum and instruction. But when it came to culture that hadn't occurred to me. I had been looking at culture as something that leaders create. I had been talking only with the principals and academic directors about it for a few years. And we had managed to make tremendous progress. But Liz was suggesting something much deeper, and with potentially sweeping consequences: why not give teachers ownership over workplace culture itself?

So Liz and I called Jason, Ajua, and a few other teachers who were in town, and we set up a meeting later in July. I shared with them everything I had been thinking about for the last few years—the belief that workplace culture can bring out the best in people, the reason we had created our values.

The ideas started flowing right away. One teacher suggested we make culture the theme for the coming Summer Institute. Another suggested that our current teachers should come up with a way to welcome our new teachers while also introducing them to our values and culture.

As I listened, it occurred to me that the teachers should lead the most important day of the most important forum of the year. So I did something we had never done before: instead of planning the opening day of Institute with my leadership team, as I'd always done in the past, I asked the teachers if they wanted to plan the agenda. They jumped at the chance.

That night I took out our values statement. I sat on the floor, leaning against the couch with my laptop in front of me on a pillow, and stared at my bookshelves. I thought about how amazing it could be if all the teachers saw themselves as owners of our culture.

As I sat there, one book caught my eye: *The Story of My Experiments with Truth*, Gandhi's classic autobiography. I heard his famous quote in my head: "Be the change you wish to see in the world."

Be the change. *Be the culture,* I thought. It reminded me of what I had written at Teachers College for my first paper: "In its highest form, education means being an embodiment of the message one wishes to communicate." I thought again about what Liz had said: It was not my job to hand down happiness. It was our collective responsibility—teachers and leaders together—to build the kind of community that we wanted to work and live in. To create the organizational culture we wanted, each of us needed to become an embodiment of our culture. We all needed to *be the culture*. That was it.

I opened our "Culture and Values" document on my laptop and started a second page. I found myself typing furiously:

Be the Culture. Who we are becomes our culture. So we
aspire to speak, think, and act in harmony with our values.
Our words, our thoughts, and our deeds collectively become
our culture—the environment in which we live and work
every day. We nurture and contribute to our culture because
it is our culture that nurtures us. And it is our culture that

enables us to do our best work and to become our best selves. So we call out (or, when necessary, counsel out, with compassion) those who do not share our values. Leadership is about values not techniques. It's a genuine love for children and families, a genuine respect for teachers. It's who you are. You can't fake it. Leaders are influential to the extent that they exemplify our values.

Then I thought about Liz's insight, and I added one last line: "We are all leaders."

At our next meeting, I shared what I had written with the teachers. They planned our Institute agenda based on our values and our new "Be the Culture" concept. The whole day would be geared toward the idea of teachers taking ownership of our workplace culture.

The first day of August was here again. I was so excited that the teachers would, for the first time ever, run Institute.

They had asked me to focus my opening remarks on the question, Why do we need to talk about culture and values?

I started by saying that I could think of at least three powerful forces that challenge our culture, and these challenges made talking about culture particularly important.

The first challenge was that most of us came from traditional public school systems, where union rulebooks, bureaucracy, and negativity dominate the workplace culture. This engenders a lack of trust and prevents both individual accountability and teamwork. We'd all come to HVA to escape those attitudes, but that default culture can still exert a powerful pull. Especially in the cold, short days of winter, we were all susceptible to the default mode of negativity and lack of accountability. As an analogy, I said, if you do sit-ups every day, you'll get stronger, but if you stop doing them, you will eventually go back to being weak. You have to keep working on the positive in order to not revert to the negative.

The second challenge to our culture was something we'd learned the hard way: negativity has disproportionate influence. Let's say you have a group of twenty-five people and twenty-two of them are positive—only three are gossiping about a colleague or complaining or not working hard. You'd think the positive would outweigh the negative. But it's a funny thing about human nature and group dynamics: Negativity is dominant. And it spreads like a virus. And people with negative energy don't usually keep it to themselves; they tend to be quite vocal. As I spoke, the teachers exchanged knowing glances.

Finally, the third challenge: "Today is the first day of Institute, so all of us are rested and feeling great," I said. "Institute is the honeymoon, and the school year is the marriage. As much as we love each other and love our kids and believe in our cause, the fall turns to winter every year, and the work gets tougher. Sooner or later we'll get stressed out. The daily frustrations can cause us to be susceptible to a negative culture."

"Today is about how we can surmount these three huge challenges. It's about how we can keep our culture, and therefore ourselves, productive and happy."

There was only one way, I said. "What teachers taught me this summer is that culture can't be top-down, that we need to work together to build the culture that we want. It's not just that the culture makes us. Each of us makes the culture. What teachers taught me is that every one of us has to embody the culture—each of us has the power to own the culture. To be the culture."

The positive energy in the room was palpable. It was a complete paradigm shift and we all felt intrigued by the concept and eager to make it a reality. If we nurture the culture, the culture will nurture us.

The agenda then included testimonials about colleagues who

embodied our values, as well as quiet time to write personal reflections on our culture, hilarious skits, and a brainstorming session on how we could deal with the daily challenges to our culture.

The entire day had been designed by the teachers to help us connect with our values and with each other, and in so doing, to understand how each of us contributes to—and is nourished by—our culture. That institute went down in HVA lore as the best ever.

Institute had inspired a lot of our teachers to reflect on their own experiences. Michelle, for example, had worked at a public school a few blocks from HVA for five years before joining us.

"I was a decent teacher. But nobody helped me," she says. "I got no support. If a child threw a bottle against the wall, the principal would either refuse to help or tell me to 'send him down' but nothing was done to fix the problem. My old school just took everything from me. It made me tired and depleted. I understood why so many smart people leave teaching. I have to admit that I stopped putting my best effort into my lessons. Finally I realized: This can't be it. How can I do this for thirty years?

"I was ready to change professions, which was devastating for me, because in my heart I wanted to be a teacher. But I didn't know what to do.

"Why does it have to be that if you're working in a public city school you're signing a death sentence? I wanted to believe it could be better.

"When I got to HVA in every conversation I heard that every teacher's story was my story. All of us had experienced the disappointment of trying to be a good teacher only to see our dreams destroyed. But here I saw what was possible in education. It blew my mind. I'm the same person and it's the same population—even some of the same exact students I used to teach in my old school.

"Here the culture allows you to be yourself. I feel respected and heard. I'm motivated to make my lessons better.

"Coming here to teach changed everything for me, not just as a teacher but as a person. All the things that had been taken away from me were given back to me: my confidence, my ambition, my love of teaching. The culture gave me back my drive to be a better teacher. And a better person.

"This school saved my life. It helped me to find happiness and peace."

In all the prior years I had felt like we were falling short: our vision and values were aspirational.

Not this year. This year, looking around the room at Institute, and listening to the teachers, I felt that we had all experienced something sacred together.

CHAPTER 16

BORN TO RISE

JUNE 25, 2011: SEVEN YEARS, 293 days, and four hours since that rainy, early morning on our first day of school. I am standing on the stage of Cooper Union's Great Hall, a historic room where great American leaders like Abraham Lincoln, Susan B. Anthony, and Frederick Douglass had articulated their dreams for our nation. Surrounding me, in caps and gowns, is the living embodiment of those dreams: the first graduating class of Harlem Village Academies.

As I looked around I saw all the familiar faces. The parents, grandparents, and siblings who had become our HVA family were beaming. New teachers and former teachers and board members were beaming. My own three kids were beaming. So were Nick, Yohana, Andrew, and Rebecca. Everyone in the hall felt unified by the powerful sense that we had built something important together. And we were all there for one reason: these children.

I walked to the podium to welcome the audience and to address our very first graduates. "We're standing here in this historic Great

Hall, and we're standing on the shoulders of giants. Each of us is here today because of others who have gone before us. We are an entire community of people who have come together because we love you, because we believe in you—and because we believe in the potential of all humanity to rise up and to become better than we were before."

I looked at them: Kareem, Brandon, Jasmine, Victoria, and the rest of the students on the stage—all my babies. All of them were about to leave for college.

"I'd like to tell you the same thing that I told my own children when they graduated high school and left me to embark on the journey you are about to make, to college and to build an independent life . . ." I paused a moment. "Please don't go!"

Everyone laughed. I was thrilled for these children who had overcome enormous challenges to push ahead in a world where only eight of every one hundred of their peers would make it to college.

"I wish I could tell you it's all going to be easy from here, and everything will be fine," I continued. "But the truth is: you will encounter difficult times. It may be in a week or in a year. The one thing that I can promise you is that we will always be here for you, that I will always be here for you. Today is not the end of high school, but the first day of your new status as the first alumni of Harlem Village Academies." With that, the crowd went wild with applause.

Then I told the students and audience about how those words in Viktor Frankl's *Man's Search for Meaning* had inspired me and had ultimately led to the founding of our academies: "It did not really matter what we expected from life, but rather what life expected from us." I hoped this idea might uplift them at some point in the future when they would inevitably face challenges of their own. "I'm telling you now that life is asking something of you. *We* are asking something of you," I said. I wanted them to see themselves as I saw them: capable, strong young leaders with a responsibility to do something meaningful with their lives.

I concluded by sharing with the graduates the same outlook that I had tried to instill in my own children as they were growing up. "You've been given a lot. And we expect a lot of you. And we love you."

Ed Lewis, our board chairman and one of the most successful African American business leaders in the country, was our commencement speaker. "Knowing my background," Ed told the audience, "some people had low expectations of me." I knew from many conversations with Ed just how extraordinary his life's journey had been. His mother had been a maid, beautician, crossing guard, and factory worker and his father had been a janitor. As a young girl, his mother had worked in the tobacco fields in Virginia, and her grandmother had been a slave. He was raised in New York and he attended public school in the Bronx.

At the University of New Mexico, Ed was one of only twelve African Americans out of eight thousand students on campus. After a stint in banking, what he really wanted was to start his own company. So in 1968 he got together with three other young men to found *Essence*, a magazine for African American women.

Early on, business was hard to come by. Executives told him they could not advertise in a magazine for black women because then white women would not want to buy their products. Ed guided the company through the bigotry and challenges of the decades that followed, and under his leadership, *Essence* grew to reach eight million readers and became one of the country's largest African American multimedia organizations.

Musician and Harlem Village Academies board member John Legend spoke as well. A product of public schools, John said the issue of educational equity was personal for him, as he had received a quality education when so many of his friends had not. In honor of our first graduating class, John had written a school song for HVA that perfectly

230 | BORN TO RISE

embodied our shared belief that all children, not just a privileged few, are born to greatness. All of us were moved by John's inspiring words.

The students sang our new school song, their sweet voices ringing out into the Great Hall.

> Roots in the soil of Harlem town
> Growing toward the open sky
> We are the seeds of hope and love,
> Excellence and pride
>
> We see the light, We hear the call
> Call of a higher dream
> Eyes on the prize of destiny
> We will not see defeat
>
> We rise up, we rise up
> We set our sights on high
> We rise up, we rise up
> Our arms embrace the sky
>
> Deep in the heart of every child
> Planted in every mind
> Lies the desire to reach the clouds
> We were born to rise
>
> We rise up, we rise up
> We set our sights on high
> We rise up, we rise up
> We all were born to rise

Eight years earlier, in this very same month, my own son was graduating from middle school. As he received his diploma, I hoped he understood how privileged he was. I hoped he would use his life for a worthy purpose. I dreamed about instilling these same values in the students of a school that I was about to open. As I watched my son graduate, I dreamed about what our Harlem graduation would be like one day. And here I stood now, together with my son and my two daughters, and our entire community of teachers, families, and supporters who had made this day possible.

And as I listened to the students singing our new school song, I felt a sense of reverence for the words: "We rise up, we rise up. We all were born to rise."

When we got together for dinner the next evening, the graduates were still flying. Everyone was excited about college, but most of them also admitted that they were nervous about going off on their own. "We've been a small family for eight years," Eugene said, "I'm scared." Victoria agreed. "I'm scared, too. A lot of us are. Every morning I felt like I was coming to my second family at school. Any time I needed help, the teachers would drop what they were doing and help me. I'm so nervous it's not going to be that way in college." I understood exactly how they felt. "Family means we're here for you forever," I told them. "Do you guys think you're getting rid of me that easily? You better visit on Thanksgiving!"

We quickly formed an alumni committee. A few students volunteered to head it up, writing down email addresses and phone numbers of fellow classmates. "Announcement!" they shouted. "The very first HVA Alumni Committee has just been formed," Destiny said. "We'll notify you of our first reunion on Facebook."

I tried my best to speak with each student individually. I whispered to Victoria that her mother would have been so proud of her. "You know what, Dr. Kenny?" she responded. "I know because my mom, she was talking to me in the hospital before she died, she said,

'You're going to do so much better than I did, so much better than your grandma did. This school is your family and you have a future.' And she said it was a blessing that I was picked in the lottery to be in the school."

Victoria's mother, before she passed away, had said to me, "The public school system almost had me convinced that my little girl would be nothing. They almost had me." And now Victoria was heading off to college. Her mother wouldn't get to see it, but her child was on her way to becoming quite *something.*

We all talked about the first day of school—that rainy September day. I was frazzled and excited, and they were tiny fifth graders who didn't know what to expect. "I was definitely not happy with all the rules. Forget it!" Kayla said.

"Oh, I remember that first day, I met Dr. Kenny on the steps and she was like, 'Hello! Good morning! How are you? What's your name?' And I was like, why is this lady asking me questions?!" The other kids cracked up.

"Remember Friday detention? I was in there every week—that's one thing I'm not gonna miss!" Kareem laughed. "True. But, honest, I will miss all of you," Eugene said.

"And I'll miss your kids, too, Dr. Kenny. They helped me learn my times tables in fifth grade!" Brandon said. "Me, too," Damon added. "Me, too, too!" Destiny laughed. "Rachel, she was always getting us into reading, and Avi, you know, he's all about math." Jasmine chimed in, "Don't forget Chava, she spent last summer tutoring me in the SATs."

Toward the end of the evening, Kareem moved closer to me. I loved this kid. He was one of the sweetest, most good-natured boys I'd ever met.

"Dr. Kenny," Kareem said, "I just want to say thank you. Thank you, because if you hadn't started this school, I'd be hanging out in the street like everybody else. Like the drug dealers outside my building. If it weren't for you, I wouldn't be on my way to college. I never would have made it."

I was about to say, "Yes, you would have!" But I stopped myself. Kareem was not nine years old anymore. He was a young man, ready to go off on his own, and he knew that I knew he was right.

Brandon had overheard us. "Me, too. I would have been on the street. There's nothing in New York—there really isn't. Let me tell you, the kids in my neighborhood, they are about to die. I can't sugarcoat it, I can't say they're 'in trouble.' If you're lucky you go to prison like half of my friends, so you won't die. If I didn't go to this school, I'd be dead, or I'd be about to die."

I couldn't contain myself. I covered my mouth with my hand as my tears started flowing uncontrollably.

Soon there was a whole circle of kids surrounding me. "Please don't cry, Dr. Kenny. You're going to make us cry!" the girls said. "I'm sorry, I can't help it," I said, drying my eyes with my sleeve. "I love you guys. I'm going to miss you so much."

"We love you, too," Victoria said.

"Group hug!" said Eugene.

This was the first summer since starting HVA that I did not feel overwhelmed by problems. We still had challenges: we were opening new elementary schools and would soon triple the size of our staff and the number of students we served. But we were no longer a startup.

That summer, as my HVA kids were getting ready for college, my own kids were all home from college. Avi had just graduated and was preparing to spend a year working for a community health organization in an African village. Chava was entering her senior year as an English major and had a summer job at a children's book publishing company, and Rachel was entering her junior year and had a child psychology internship at Teachers College. We were all in the city together.

Steve and Ronnie, my two summer camp friends, called in July to tell me that Mel would be in the country for two weeks. We made a plan to have dinner together. We laughed and talked the whole way to New Jersey.

When we got out of the car, there Mel stood in a friend's yard. His hair might have been a bit grayer and his walk a bit slower, but he was the same old Mel to me, as he punched Ronnie in the arm and cracked me up by using the F-word even at age eighty-four. At one point as we sat together at a nearby diner we broke out into one of our favorite camp songs.

I savored every moment sitting across from Mel. When I was thirteen years old, he had told me and my friends that we could change the world, and we had embraced it. As he talked about politics and reminisced about the 1960s, I asked him to tell me more about the March on Washington. And I discovered something incredible: Mel had actually walked together with Martin Luther King for a brief moment, they had clasped hands while singing "We shall overcome."

I had trouble getting a word in edgewise, what with everyone laughing at old camp stories. But I was afraid to let this chance slide by, so I took Mel's hand for a minute to get his attention. "Mel, I just need you to know how important you were—you are—to me," I said.

"I'm so proud of you, Debbie!" he said. Normally when someone said something like that, I brushed it aside. But coming from Mel, I cherished his words. He had taught me to be a leader. And he had been my inspiration when I said to our children on our second day of school: you are the leader of your life.

Master teachers like Mel do more than impart information. They instill in students a burning desire to want to learn, and to care.

Mel was still an influence on my life decades after he'd been my teacher. It was a testament to the impact a teacher could have, the way a teacher could shape a life, and change the world.

THE EDUCATION MANIFESTO

When I started Harlem Village Academies ten years ago, I kept hearing the same question again and again: What is your school design? From the beginning, I rejected the question. I believed then, as I do now, that schools are not products to be designed and replicated. Instead, I was sure the only way to fix public education was for schools to attract, support, and motivate talented people. The question I wanted to answer was: how do we give every child in our nation an excellent teacher?

For the next ten years, I was obsessed with figuring it out.

During those same ten years the national conversation about education has permanently shifted. The days of blaming poverty, parents, or a particular curriculum are over. It is now widely understood that talented people—high quality teachers—matter more to a child's education than any other factor. And so, most everyone who cares about public education is now asking the same question: How do we give every child in our nation an excellent teacher? In other words: how do we attract and develop talent?

Talented people drive results, innovate, and push past obstacles. And talented people, working together, can turn idealistic visions and even the most challenging goals into reality. This is what has happened at Harlem Village Academies. Our teachers light up with entrepreneurial drive, and they have produced stunning student achievement results.

The importance of passionate, talented people will be obvious to anyone who has ever run anything—a business, a sports franchise, or an organization of any size. Indeed, attracting talent and building a team is the only way an enterprise can be effective. Yet in education a staggering number of roadblocks prevent schools from effectively cultivating talent.

For one thing, most state certification requirements limit whom a school can hire: a college professor with a Ph.D. in math would not be permitted to teach in most public schools. Even more detrimental are the union rules, which basically kill off any chance of cultivating talent since they guarantee jobs for life regardless of teacher quality. The rules also prevent principals from making basic management decisions regarding hiring, firing, and evaluating their teams.

As a result of these barriers, our public schools have been failing on a massive scale that is steadily weakening our economy as well as the social fabric of our country. In 1983, the situation had become so dire that a landmark presidential commission asserted that if a foreign nation "had attempted to impose on America the mediocre educational performance that exists today, we might well have viewed it as an act of war." Today, almost three decades later, the situation is still abysmal. There is not a single city in America where all public school students are passing even the most basic exams in reading and math. Not one. Picture a child entering kindergarten: if she has been born into poverty, she stands only an 8 percent chance of making it to college.

How did we get here? And what can we do to turn our schools into inspiring learning communities that raise children to become sophisticated, independent thinkers who care about the world and contribute to society?

We got here by disrespecting teachers.

The rules-based system created by unions and politicians protects incompetent teachers and creates a bureaucratic working environment that is so frustrating to the majority of dedicated teachers that many leave the profession in their prime. These rules have created a culture that disrespects teachers by refusing to allow them to be held accountable in the same manner other professionals are. Worst of all, the rules have cemented the treatment of teachers as low-level workers: When there is no accountability, workers are inevitably told exactly how to do their jobs. They are not given the freedom and respect that define being a professional. This undermines the teamwork that is essential to running a great school.

Imagine the Ritz-Carlton, Google, Facebook, or any university creating a system that did not allow their managers to manage—to make basic decisions, such as who is hired, fired, promoted, and so on. It would be absurd. Principals, like all managers, must be empowered to evaluate their teachers and nurture their teams. In other words, principals must be allowed to *lead*. The school district, in turn, should evaluate principals based on the whole school's performance, including test scores and other measures, and hold them directly accountable for results.

Critics will claim that in this model principals could fire effective teachers based on favoritism, which is a reasonable concern and one that should be addressed. But there are many ways to prevent or remedy this, such as blind staff and parent surveys, whole school inspections, and other rigorous principal-evaluation measures. More important, these critics would defend a system that goes to great lengths to protect an adult from losing a job yet ignores the protection of innocent children. Further, if the evaluation of principals and their very job security depended on school results, most would do everything in their power to build a positive culture that supports and retains great teachers.

The importance of teacher and principal empowerment cannot be overstated: human judgment should not be removed from schools, because education is a profoundly human enterprise. Consider the example of one of our teachers, Steve, who came to Harlem Village Academies with several years of experience at a public school. In his first year at HVA, he struggled with everything from student behavior to lesson planning, confiding in me that he knew his performance was "mediocre at best." Our principal, Sam, had observed Steve struggling but he'd also gotten to know Steve during faculty retreats and workouts and saw that he was smart, capable, and embraced our values of accountability and hard work. In Sam's judgment, Steve had the potential for significant improvement, so Sam took him to dinner and offered encouragement and practical pointers that motivated Steve to improve. Steve was grateful for the support. "I'll remember that conversation for perhaps the rest of my life," he said. "It made me feel hopeful. I was wonderstruck."

Steve went on to become a top performer. Not only did 100 percent of his eighth graders score proficient on the state math test, but 100 percent also passed the high school Regents exam one year in advance. If the principal had been busy complying with checklists imposed by a government bureaucracy, he would not have been able to cultivate Steve's potential. Steve would have likely received a poor rating from outside experts that would have demoralized him to the point that he would have left the profession entirely. America's schools would have lost another great teacher.

And it is great teachers that make a school great. Harlem Village Academies regularly hosts visitors from around the country who say they are blown away by what they see: it's not just a few amazing teachers, but entire schools filled with intensely passionate professionals who teach at a high level while having fun. Visitors come away feeling they have experienced something remarkable and talking about a special feeling in our schools that they say is virtually impossible to describe. Some are even brought to tears. That's because what they are seeing when they observe our teachers is transcendent: it is the human spirit soaring to its highest potential.

We are constantly asked by these visitors, including many school leaders, how they can achieve the same. They start by asking about our curriculum, our teaching practices, and behavior systems, and we happily share all that we know. But we always share it with a caveat: It's our people and culture that generate the results. Our educational methods work because our teachers have been entrusted to select or develop them. "Proven" methods imposed on a group of teachers who have no ownership and are not motivated to carry them out will fall flat.

And while our teachers are given the freedom to innovate, much of what they do is not new at all; they often draw on the work of readily available curriculum and research. Every school in America has access to the same pedagogical ideas and methods we use. The problem is not a lack of information, but a lack of motivation engendered by the low accountability/low empowerment culture in our public schools. As management guru Peter Drucker explained, knowledge worker productivity is fundamentally dependent on the *attitude* of the knowledge worker.

We spent years thinking deeply about how to design our schools to attract and nurture talented people, and it all came down to creating a workplace culture of learning, team, and ownership. We created a culture of learning where teachers collaborate to continually improve their practice; a culture of team where teachers are supported, respected, appreciated, and have a blast together; and a culture of ownership where teachers have more than just a voice—they are trusted to make important decisions, then held accountable for results. Our ideas about people and culture sound obvious, yet our culture has become so powerful that people feel drawn to it and transformed by it. So powerful, in fact, that it turns mediocre performance into great performance.

But is this scalable? Can focusing on talent dramatically improve the failing school systems in Chicago, Oakland, or Washington, D.C.? Can focusing on talent transform public education in America? The answer is no.

And yes—but only if we radically shift our approach.

Everything we have learned and accomplished at Harlem Village Academies has been enabled by two conditions: accountability and freedom. These two conditions—which are the essence of charter schools—do not guarantee success, but they are an absolute prerequisite to enabling any school to be successful. Why? Because accountability enables freedom, and freedom unleashes teacher passion.

As a charter, we're given freedom from bureaucratic union rules. We can pass on that freedom to our teachers because they are willing to be held accountable for results as professionals. So we get clear on objectives and get out of the way. Our teachers love it! They come up with their own ideas or select whichever practices they think are best. It's great for children, parents, and the majority of teachers. The only losers are truly unqualified teachers.

What needs to happen next is clear. Teachers, parents, and concerned citizens must pressure policy makers to enact policies that treat teachers and principals as professionals: give them freedom to do their jobs and hold them accountable for results. No compromise position will work—it will continue to frustrate great teachers and discourage new talent from entering the profession.

American public schools are filled with dedicated teachers whose morale is being destroyed by a low-accountability, low-empowerment culture that disrespects them. The fight for education reform will continue to be tough, but I am confident we will get there. When the forces that are now protecting the status quo finally come around to doing what's best for children, they will find that it is also what's best for the majority of teachers.

Then we will see the brightest minds competing for the privilege of working in the teaching profession, which will finally be elevated to its rightful place as the noblest profession in our nation. And then every school will become a place where teachers become their best selves and in turn inspire their students so that they may rise up to reach their own highest potential.

ACKNOWLEDGMENTS

An incredible community of people has come together over the last ten years to create, nurture, and build the dream that is Harlem Village Academies. There is no way to fully express the depth of my gratitude to the numerous individuals who have given their time, love, and energy to help our students and to further the cause of educational equity.

Above all I want to thank our talented teachers: You are the heroes of this book and of this country. You inspire me every day with your passion and drive and your commitment to our shared vision.

I am so grateful for the dedication of our principals and leaders. You are the best there is. Thank you for your partnership and friendship, and for always putting the children and teachers first.

My sincere appreciation to every single member of our support team. Thank you for dedicating your lives to the greater good. Nothing—literally—would work without you.

To our students: You were born to greatness. Your strong minds and tender hearts remind us how lucky we are to teach you and learn from you.

To our wonderful families—parents, grandparents, guardians—thank you for your goodwill and trust. We are so proud of your children.

One of the great privileges of my life has been to work with the board of Harlem Village Academies, an extraordinary group of successful, busy individuals who ask for nothing more than the chance to make a difference. Thank you for your service.

To our incredibly generous supporters, volunteers, and mentors: thank you for your kindness and for enabling us to provide a quality education for Harlem's children.

My profound thanks to the business leaders and trusted advisors who have taken the time to provide me with guidance over the years.

Thank you to my education reform colleagues throughout the country whose generosity of spirit has helped me and many others. It is an honor to work in this movement alongside activists and educators who power through every day to keep fighting the good fight.

This project began in May 2009 and many people helped with its development.

Thank you to Nathan Myhrvold, who first suggested that I write this book and insisted that it had to be personal. Thank you to John Legend, for writing the school song that inspired the title of the book.

This book would not exist without Bari Weiss, whose masterful editing was indispensable. Thank you for your patience and remarkable fortitude.

It has been an absolute delight to work with Hollis Heimbouch, my brilliant editor at HarperCollins. I could not have written this book without your valuable insights and thoughtful feedback.

Thank you to Brian Murray and Jonathan Burnham at HarperCollins for your enthusiasm and support. Thank you as well to Colleen Lawrie, Jamie Brickhouse, Kathy Schneider, Leah Wasielewski, Leslie Cohen, Lisa Stokes, Mark Ferguson, Richard Ljoenes, Stephanie Selah, Tina Andreadis, and Tom Pitoniak at HarperCollins for all your hard work and dedication.

A special thank-you to Bob Barnett for your guidance and commitment to this book and our mission.

My heartfelt gratitude to Mary Lebitz for your uncanny ability to notice every detail and your belief that everything matters. And for making me laugh whenever I was about to cry!

Many thanks to Andrew Mandel, Ayana Byrd, Dan Coleman, David Black, Grace McQuade, Joe Brenner, Karen Gottlieb, Lynn Goldberg, Michael Shnayerson, Robert Goldstein, Tanya McKinnon, and everyone who read the manuscript and offered advice.

It takes a village to raise a child and I have been blessed beyond measure by the support of my family and so many friends. Thank you to my parents, Len and Renee; my sister, Alisa, and her family, Chuck, Jessica, and Ben; the Kenny family, Bob, Shirley, David, Dan, Jon, Sarah, and Maddie; and my extended family for your unconditional love.

My three children, Avi, Chava, and Rachel, have been by my side throughout the entire process of writing this book, as they are throughout everything. You make me so proud and happy; I am the luckiest mom in the world.

Finally: to the millions of teachers and individuals who work hard every day without acknowledgement for the sake of our nation's children, I offer my humble gratitude.